Advance Praise

"My team paid tens of thousands of dollars to work with Claire and Gia, and we earned every dollar back tenfold. This book shows exactly how they did it and how you can too."

—RAND FISHKIN, FOUNDER AT SPARKTORO

"Taking a customer-focused approach to growth sounds like common sense, but there aren't many resources that actually unpack the process of how to do it. Forget The Funnel gives leaders a practical, step-by-step guide to building an impactful growth strategy and connecting the dots between strategy and daily work. It also includes dozens of real-life case studies, examples, and concrete ideas you can move on in the same day. A very high ROI book."

—LENNY RATCHITSKY, WRITER, INVESTOR, AND PRODUCT ADVISOR

"'Talk to your customers' is problematic advice coming from most people. Not Gia and Claire. I've seen a lot of startups doing haphazard research leading to questionable marketing and sales tactics. This book is the antidote to that. If you need a systematic way to understand your customers and a methodology to apply that knowledge for higher-impact messaging, marketing, and growth, this book is for you."

—APRIL DUNFORD, AUTHOR OF *OBVIOUSLY AWESOME*

"Everyone has an instinct around listening to your customers and learning to leverage their insights in your product. But it's only after reading Gia and Claire's book that you come away with the full process. Those who do it will have a measurable advantage over those who are winging it. This is the new gold standard, and the questions in chapter three will be memorized by product and product marketing teams from now on. I'm going to have to give this book to every product team I lead and every coaching client I have."

—CHRIS LEMA, CHIEF PRODUCT OFFICER AND COACH

"Great marketing starts with knowing your customer. The best marketers don't just start with the channel they know best or try a trending tactic; they build a foundational understanding of their customers and let strategy flow from there. Read this book for a crash course on how to do this well, and you'll get more impact out of your marketing efforts."

—EMILY KRAMER, CO-FOUNDER AT MKT1 AND
FORMER ADVISOR FOR CARTA AND ASANA

"Marketing for SaaS products is a special beast. Sometimes you feel like banging your head against the wall, because traditional 'channels' and 'funnels' don't work. Gia and Claire teach you how to unlock customer insights and how exactly to apply them in your marketing (exercises and examples included). This book is chicken soup for a SaaS marketer's soul."

—JANE PORTMAN, CO-FOUNDER AT USERLIST
AND FOUNDER AT UI BREAKFAST

"Forget the Funnel is a must-read book for anyone who wants to unlock explosive growth for their business. It's especially true for PLG companies because you can't be truly product-led if you're not first customer-led. In this book, Gia and Claire reveal the step-by-step and battle-tested framework that they've used with SaaS companies like Unbounce, Calendly, FullStory, Wistia, and so many more. This book will inspire and equip you with actionable steps to take, critical changes to make, and processes to improve, all geared to deliver a world-class customer experience. Don't just buy just one book. Buy it for your team, your whole company, and any colleagues you want to succeed!"

—RAMLI JOHN, AUTHOR OF *PRODUCT-LED ONBOARDING*

"This book is a must-read for anyone in SaaS. All too often, teams of all sizes struggle with having a million things to do but only one or two that truly matter. Figuring out what that 'one thing' is, however, can seem impossible. This book will offer you practical tips, strategic insights, and real examples that will help fast-track your growth beyond any best practice or hack. Stop guessing, and pick up this book immediately. You won't put it down!"

—TARA ROBERTSON, CMO AT BITLY AND FORMER CMO AT TEAMWORK, SPROUT SOCIAL, AND HOTJAR

"What you're holding in your hands is years of practical experience of not one but two skilled marketing leaders: Gia and Claire. This highly actionable book perfectly lays out their unique knowledge of customer-led growth. If you want to reduce the guesswork in your marketing and gain more decision-making confidence, this book is an absolute must-read."

—TIM SOULO, CMO AT AHREFS

"Some things are greater than the sum of their parts, and the customer-led growth framework Gia and Claire have built is one of them. Combining their backgrounds and years of expertise into one repeatable process is like 1 + 1 = 3. An essential read for anyone in charge of growing and scaling a business."

—ALLISON ESPOSITO MEDINA, CEO AND FOUNDER OF TECH LADIES AND FORMER MANAGER AT GOOGLE

"This book elevates marketing from a sum of tactics to the strategic process it deserves to be. Implementing the Customer-Led Growth Framework democratizes customer understanding, creates a shared language for your team, and unlocks the best ideas—because you're unlocking all of the brains at your company. It'll be my go-to playbook for years to come."

—MARGARET KELSEY, MARKETING COACH, FORMERLY WITH OPENVIEW, APPCUES, AND INVISION

"Everyone says to 'talk to your customers,' but no one really understands the operational challenges of doing it like Gia and Claire. They've helped dozens of companies run customer discovery and, crucially, turn the insights gathered into marketing campaigns that move the needle.

"Forget storytelling, the hero's journey, etc.—which make you want to scratch your head and say, 'But I sell a SaaS product, not a Hollywood script.' Gia and Claire's Customer-Led Growth Framework is what we've been missing in modern marketing. They present hard data and concrete examples of how to gather (and operationalize) insights to unlock revenue growth. I'll be sending copies of this book to my team, my friends, and our customers."

—KAMIL REXTIN, GM AT 42AGENCY

"Having worked directly with Claire and her team, I've seen the application of these principles firsthand (64% increase in product adoption and 300% increase in ongoing product usage). As marketers and product leaders, we often need a fresh set of eyes to help us navigate the next opportunity for growth. Reading Forget the Funnel will surely help you to see new opportunities for predictable and sustainable growth."

—DERIK SUTTON, CMO AT AUTOBOOKS

"Gia and Claire's expertise shines through in Forget the Funnel. They've done this before, and we get to learn from their years implementing this framework in the real world with real clients. I highly recommend it."

—BRIAN SUN, SENIOR GROWTH MANAGER AT TITAN, FORMERLY WITH OPENDOOR AND AUTOPILOT

Forget the Funnel

A customer-led
approach for driving
predictable,
recurring revenue

Forget

THE

FUNNEL

**georgiana laudi &
claire suellentrop**

LIONCREST
PUBLISHING

FORGET THE FUNNEL
A Customer-Led Approach for Driving
Predictable, Recurring Revenue

FIRST EDITION

ISBN   978-1-5445-4223-2   *Paperback*
          978-1-5445-4224-9   *Ebook*
          978-1-5445-4225-6   *Audiobook*

*To the friends and early believers whose support and influence
fueled the development of our process (and this book).*

Extra thanks to the Shine Crew.

*Extra, extra thanks to our unshakeable
partners for always being in our corner.*

(From Gia: For my daughters, who can do anything.)

CONTENTS

FOREWORD

—Bob Moesta, author and co-architect of the Jobs-to-be-Done Framework

I am so honored and humbled to write this foreword for Claire and Gia's book, *Forget the Funnel*. They have both directly and indirectly impacted my approach and skills in marketing products and services, taking me to a much deeper level. This is saying a lot as a very nerdy engineer who did not appreciate the work, creativity, and processes required for marketing when I started out my career. I am a changed person because of them.

Growing up I was the boy in my garage always tinkering around, trying to make something out of nothing. I'd spend hours sorting through discarded junk and scrap—broken TVs, arc welders, pumps, speakers—taking them down to their bits and pieces and transforming other people's trash into my new creations. I love to build new things.

Engineering was a natural fit for my career. Marketing and sales, not so much.

However, about twenty years ago, that all changed. I had the opportunity to lead sales and marketing for a local home builder in southwestern Michigan. I thought at the time that it couldn't be that hard. Boy, I was wrong!

Immediately I set out to learn the ropes from the experts— our top sales and marketing people in the industry. They organized a focus group of active buyers, and I diligently took notes.

"What do you want in a new house?" the group facilitator asked.

The group of buyers got specific: a finished basement, upgraded windows, stainless steel appliances, an Energy Star-compliant home. Energy Star compliance topped everyone's list; we heard it once, twice, by the end we heard it ten times.

Great, I thought! *We'll upgrade the homes to become Energy Star compliant.*

It wasn't a simple task. We needed specific windows, insulation, and an upgraded furnace and air conditioner. Even the homes' foundations had to change. It took six months of procurement time, adding options to the system, training salespeople, etc., but we were finally able to offer the option.

The response: crickets. No one bought our Energy Star-compliant homes. I was completely perplexed. *What's happening here?* I wondered.

I'd been letting the experts lead, as well as listening to what buyers *said* they wanted. And that clearly hadn't worked, so I decided to go back to my roots—jobs to be done in innovation—and listen to why someone *really* bought a house. I wanted to separate what people *said* from what they actually *did.*

So I pulled up a chair and listened as a top salesperson closed a deal. Now, our homes were typically starter homes, perfect for a young family or older generations downsizing. The moment the buyer understood the price—Energy Star compliance costs about the same as a finished basement—they chose to prioritize the finished basement over Energy Star compliance every time. *Huh, that's interesting,* I thought.

Then I took my handy flip chart and sat down with homeowners who'd recently purchased one of our houses. One after another, I heard the same thing: as much as they *aspired* to have an Energy Star-compliant home, when push came to shove, that's not what they picked.

The "experts" had gotten it all wrong; I started to see a different way forward, one led by customers. I really wish I'd had this book back then. It would have saved me so much time and effort, as well as made us more successful.

I met Claire a few years ago at a conference, where she gave a presentation on how she and Gia incorporate Jobs-to-be-Done (JTBD) into their approach to marketing. I marveled at the incredibly practical approach they took, focused on the customer as opposed to trying to sell. It felt almost engineering-like. We quickly became fast friends and colleagues, and since then, I've watched her and Gia in action garnering tremendous results, helping companies grow, and building their business and community. They're able to uncover what customers *really* value and turn it into results and growth for businesses.

The process of acquiring and retaining a high-value customer requires insight into both the problem space and the solution space. Marketing is an essential component of getting people to be aware that they even have a problem—push—and that there is a solution to help them make progress. If you want to sell, you better get into the buyer's head and understand their world from their perspective. Claire and Gia will teach you how to do that.

If you've read my book *Demand Side Sales 101*, then you'll understand when I say that *Forget the Funnel* is probably the sister book to it; if I were to name this book, I'd call *Demand Side Marketing 101*. It's incredible! Once you see it, you can't unsee it. Enjoy.

Part I

FORGETTING THE FUNNEL

Chapter 1

WHY YOU SHOULD READ THIS BOOK

When I (Gia) was leading marketing at a growing SaaS (Software as a Service) company, I often described my work style as "running around like a chicken with its head cut off." Even though I'm strategic by nature, I struggled *daily* to keep my head above water. I was desperate to demonstrate results to my stakeholders, my team, and myself. I thought that as the person responsible for driving new growth, I'd be letting everyone down if I didn't hit—or ideally surpass—my targets.

There was an endless list of tactics I needed to implement. Tactics based on what I was seeing other companies do, channels that were trending at the time, and things that'd worked for me at previous companies I'd worked with.

I worked *looong* hours—sometimes with only incremental proof that what I was doing was working. Another blog post, another webinar, another feature announcement. Marketing based on a list of tactics like this felt like running experiments in petri dishes: a bunch of little gelatinous circles with bits tossed in and tweaked as we stared at them, looking for the smallest indicator that something, *anything*, was working.

Running marketing experiments like this became my life. I was determined to make an impact, to impress the team. Work took over everything.

And that's the mode I stayed in for over a year, worried about hitting targets, drumming up ideas last minute, and spreading out campaigns to hit goals one month to the next.

I knew it wasn't sustainable. I knew I needed to hire more help. But I barely had time to get a job posted, let alone run interviews and onboard new team members. So the marketing experiments continued, and I kept running around overwhelmed, frustrated, unable to get the hell out of my own way.

Around that time, while in San Francisco for a conference, something happened that completely shifted my thinking. A light bulb moment. **I went from obsessing over typical marketing metrics like traffic and leads, to centering my view of growth on measuring customer value.**

You'll get the full story in a later chapter, but for now, here's what you need to know: that experience paved the way for what Claire (the co-author of this book) and I now refer to as "customer-led growth." It's how I stopped marketing in panic mode, and how our team at that growing SaaS company increased revenue by nearly 900% in the next two years—

with only a seed round of funding and no reliance on paid acquisition channels.

THE PROBLEM

This struggle is not unique. Many marketing teams operate in a haphazard way, flinging ideas around like spaghetti, trying to see what sticks. But scrambling like this is no way to generate long-term growth. In fact, **it *prevents* sustainable and predictable growth.** Most marketing teams don't have time to stop, look around, and ask themselves, "Why isn't this working?"

Let's make this a little more personal. Maybe it's *your* team running around, stressed and exhausted. Perhaps the person responsible for marketing and growth—whether that's you or a member of your team—has tried what feels like everything to more predictably drive new traffic, leads, and signups. Maybe you've spent months working on content marketing and thought leadership pieces. Thrown money at paid social and search campaigns. Tweaked and optimized the funnel every way you can think of.

And still, revenue growth is...lumpy. Slow. Inconsistent. The arrow on the chart goes up and to the right *some* months, but other months, it dips again and no one can really point to why.

So you go with what you know: *more* tactics to generate *more* leads to bring in *more* sales—in effect, more petri dishes. More shots in the dark. More spaghetti on the wall. Pick your metaphor.

It's not that your ideas are bad or wrong. Your company *needs* to invest time and resources into marketing, just as it needs to invest in product, customer support, sales, and engineering.

The *real* problem is, **you're guessing.**

THE SOLUTION

Many teams think they'll find the solution to their marketing challenges by listening to the experts or learning from what others have done. But **what worked for someone else, at some other company, with some other target audience isn't automatically relevant to *your* business, *your* product, or *your* customers.** As a result, applying most marketing advice actually leads to more chaos and more uninformed experiments.

The information you *actually* need to fix inconsistent, unpredictable growth is found in one place: **inside your best customers' heads.**

Specifically, you need to understand:

- what life was like for your customers *before* they started using your solution;
- what happened that made them realize, "*This isn't working. I need something else;*"
- what they did *next*, and *next*, and *next*, until they found you;
- what led them to choose *you* over all the other options;
- what *value* they experienced that convinced them to pay for your solution;

- what they're able to do *now* that they weren't able to do before; and
- what happened next—that is, how they've *changed* and *grown* as they've been your customer.

Once you know all of this, **you'll have everything you need to build a marketing (and product and sales) strategy that actually moves the needle.**

You'll know what to say in your marketing campaigns, what channels to use, and what parts of your product to highlight for potential customers, in what order. As a result, you'll reach and resonate with more right-fit customers and see more consistent growth.

We know: the idea of "getting inside your best customers' heads" might not sound like a tangible solution to the enormous pressure you're feeling to hit your goals. You needed a solution *yesterday*.

But hear us out: this insight is the first step away from the chaos, toward 900% revenue growth. And as you'll see in this book, **it actually *is* quite tangible, and it doesn't *have* to be some big, complicated, or expensive thing.**

This book will show you exactly how to:

- **Learn from your customers and turn that data into real insight (covered in Part II).** You'll extract their struggles, anxieties, motivations, "aha" moments, and desired outcomes. You'll take the data you've gathered and analyze it to identify your best customers, what they value, and why they chose *you* (hint: it might not be what you think).

- **Map and measure your customer's experience (covered in Part III).** You'll map the actions, touchpoints, motivations, and objections throughout their relationship with you. You'll know what creates value for your ideal customers and finally measure what matters: that is, the KPIs (key performance indicators) that will tell you you've done *your* job helping customers achieve theirs.
- **Find your biggest levers for growth and build alignment (covered in Part IV).** You'll identify your customer's success gaps, get clear on how you'll bridge those gaps, and make shit happen. You'll finally be able to align your team's efforts with measurable targets that translate to happier, higher lifetime value customers.

We call this three-phase process the **Customer-Led Growth Framework** (Figure 1.1). It's the method we use to help companies—of all sizes and at all stages of growth—calm the marketing chaos and hit ambitious revenue targets.

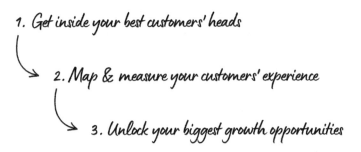

Figure 1.1. The three stages of the Customer-Led Growth Framework

HOW WE GOT HERE

Hey, Claire here. While Gia was leading marketing at Unbounce (that fast-growing startup), I was cutting my teeth in the SaaS industry after working as a marketer in other fields. I'd joined an early-stage startup called Calendly as the second employee. As the Director of Marketing, I was ready to tackle the typical early-stage startup challenges: building awareness of a product no one had heard of yet, generating demand, and acquiring initial customers.

But it quickly became clear that Calendly didn't have the typical "build awareness and generate demand" problems. Instead, our challenge was *activating* the many free signups coming in each day, and converting more of those free users into paying customers. My focus shifted away from traditional marketing metrics like website visits and free signups, toward more product-focused metrics like new user activation and free-to-paid conversion rates.

While trying to figure out how to move the needle on these metrics, I stumbled upon the Jobs-to-be-Done (JTBD) theory: a research process that helps uncover a customer's motivation for buying a product.

JTBD put words to a concept that I understood but couldn't explain before: that people "hire" a solution to improve their life in some way, and they "fire" that solution when it no longer serves them.

Through a *shit* ton of customer interviews, I uncovered the reasons our best customers hired our product. I used these insights to build new customer onboarding programs for the different reasons customers hired us; support docs that helped customers best leverage the product based on what they wanted to accomplish; case studies highlighting the different ways Calendly provided value—the list goes on.

By the time I was ready to move on from the company and switch to solo consulting, we'd grown from pre-revenue to $4 million in ARR (annual recurring revenue). In a wild coincidence, as with Gia's story, this hypergrowth *also* happened in just two years, with only a seed round of funding and no reliance on paid acquisition channels.

As a new freelancer, I quickly became overwhelmed with demand from SaaS founders and execs *desperate* to find marketers who'd weathered the journey from startup to scaleup. In a then-small community (*shoutout to Tech Ladies*), I saw a post from Gia, who'd also left her in-house role. She was experiencing the same level of demand that I was, and was looking to connect with collaborators. Obviously, I jumped in.

* * *

We met in person for the first time at a conference in Boston. On the last day, we sat in the lobby of a hotel and bought the domain name forgetthefunnel.com.

Why "forget the funnel"? **Because the traditional concept of a "marketing funnel" has no place in recurring revenue business models like SaaS.** The concept of a marketing funnel (Figure 1.2) only accounts for a customer searching for and purchasing a new solution—but to be successful, recurring revenue-based businesses need customers to *continue paying* month after month, year after year.

Figure 1.2. The "old way": the traditional marketing and sales funnel

If your business runs on recurring revenue, it's a *serious* mistake to think about marketing as something that stops when someone signs up.

In 2017, we launched our Forget the Funnel video workshop series. Forget the Funnel wasn't originally a business; it was a joint project to help marketers in the tech and SaaS world. We wanted to give them the support their companies typically couldn't.

While running Forget the Funnel together, we realized we

each held a piece of the scalable growth puzzle: Claire's expertise comes from years of helping SaaS companies gather deep customer insights and uncover their customers' jobs-to-be-done. Meanwhile, Gia's expertise is the result of having operationalized customer value to help high-growth companies rapidly scale their marketing programs and their teams.

Simply put, Claire knows how to *get* the critical insight needed to inform an impactful growth strategy; Gia knows how to *apply* it.

Two years later, prompted by an influx of companies needing both skill sets, we joined forces. We grafted our methods into one cohesive, repeatable process and gave it a name.

To date, the Customer-Led Growth Framework has helped thousands of marketers, founders, execs, and consultants get out of the weeds, think more strategically about marketing, and meaningfully impact revenue growth.

HOW THIS BOOK CAN HELP YOU

Our mission in writing this book is the same as the mission of our business: to help companies, especially in tech, be more customer-led—because it helps them deliver more value, be more successful, and be better places to work and grow.

This book will *not* give you a toolbox of tactics "guaranteed" to drive growth. You already know enough tactics.

Rather than a toolbox, this book will give you a *blueprint* for growth, so you can *choose* the tools that are actually right for your company, your team, and your customers.

This book will help you make better decisions about what to implement, when, and how. You'll have a *system* for making these decisions and reaching more predictable, meaningful growth. You'll get out of the haphazard cycle so many companies get stuck in. Getting out *will* require a shift in how you operate—but ultimately, it will relieve the time and energy burden by giving your team clear direction.

And good news: **marketing problems may have brought you to this book, but solving them will actually end up benefiting your entire business.**

We recommend that you read this book all the way through once. It can *fundamentally change* the way you run your business. Once you're done, pass it on to your team (more on who we mean by "your team" in Chapter 2). They'll use it as their guide while applying the Customer-Led Growth Framework.

Chapters include real examples, how to apply customer-led growth to your situation, and a "Your Turn" section recapping how to take action. You'll also see mentions of follow-on resources we've created to help your team implement: meeting agendas, worksheets, templates, and so on. You can get all of those resources at forgetthefunnel.com/workbook (anytime we direct you to "the workbook," this is what we're referring to).

In the next chapter, we'll start by helping you create a cross-functional team to ensure the best possible success, in the shortest amount of time.

YOUR TURN

Imagine your customer back before they'd ever heard of your product. They don't know you, and they don't know they need you.

One day, something happens that leads them to realize, "This isn't working. I can't live like this anymore," and their search for a new solution begins. How does this search play out for your customer? How do you cut through the noise and make your solution the obvious choice?

It's the documentary of "How I Met Your Product" through your customer's eyes.

Think about how much more effective you could be at reaching, resonating with, and *retaining* great-fit customers if you knew more about their psychology—why they do what they do (covered in Part II of this book). You'd know where to find the customers who want to find you—hell, who will be grateful to find you. You'd be more effective at showing them you're the answer to their problems, helping them adopt your tool, reach value, and become a customer for life (covered in Part III of this book).

This book will help you be a better matchmaker.

If you're at all unclear on who that customer is, the words they use, what triggered their search for a new solution, how to find them, what their deal breakers are, or what their "aha" moment looked like, please *keep reading*.

Chapter 2

BUILDING YOUR CUSTOMER-LED TEAM

When Tara Robertson joined Sprout Social, a social media management SaaS, the company had just raised their Series C funding round. Sprout serves many different customer segments: small businesses, the mid-market, enterprise companies, and agencies—each of which has its own unique pain points and needs.

Agencies were their most unpredictable segment in terms of how long they'd stick around as customers. So to increase retention, Sprout planned to launch a revenue-share program: essentially, agencies could get a small cut of the subscription revenue generated by new customers *they* referred to Sprout Social. At the time, several well-known SaaS companies were successfully running programs like this. Implementing one at Sprout seemed like a logical move.

When Tara came on board, her first mission was to build this new program from the ground up. So she created a plan, got the buy-in needed to make a full-time hire (Luke), and together they were off to the races.

Tara and Luke *could've* just copied the model others were using—but instead, they turned to Sprout's customers first. **Through customer surveys and interviews, they learned that agencies using Sprout *weren't* all that motivated by the revenue-share opportunity; what they *really* wanted was community.** Agency owners wanted help crafting scalable, profitable service offerings for their clients. They wanted to tap into a network of fellow agency professionals. They wanted to collaborate with brands (like Sprout!) to get in front of more potential clients and win more business.

Building what customers *wanted* would be a departure from building what company leaders had envisioned. Tara knew that to win buy-in for this new direction, she'd need to make a compelling case, then keep the leadership team informed and engaged every step of the way.

She presented the surprising findings and—*hooray*—got approval to move forward. She and Luke recruited 100 agency customers to take part in a beta program as founding members. These customers were at the core of the program strategy, sharing feedback, engaging with content, and providing insights on which parts of the program were most valuable.

Tara continued keeping company leaders involved and engaged at each step, knowing that this would lock upper-level buy-in and give Sprout's new Agency Partner Program legs.

As agencies participated in the program, their businesses began to grow—and as they grew, so did their use of Sprout. **Churn dropped substantially, and expansion sales from agency customers increased the company's ARR by $2.1 million, *all within just six months.***

* * *

It might seem like the most important part of this story is the significant ARR lift in just months. Actually, what's most important is that they never would have achieved such a significant lift, had Tara tried to go it alone.

To successfully implement the Customer-Led Growth Framework, there must be buy-in and alignment from teams across the organization—and senior leadership needs to, well, *lead* the way.

So let's build your team.

ADVANTAGES OF A CROSS-FUNCTIONAL TEAM

To create *and sustain* change, you'll need to form a cross-functional team. The team doesn't have to be huge, but buy-in from multiple departments is needed. **Here's why:**

1. **Working cross-functionally leverages each department's existing knowledge.** Product, Sales, Marketing, and, of course, Customer Success all think about customers a *lot*. They all work directly with customers and have valuable insight about your customer's experience that they can bring to the table.

2. **It gets each department invested in the project's success.** When a person directly influences a project, they care more about the success of that project. Contribution builds ownership. It helps team members see themselves and the role they play in the customer's experience.
3. **It increases collaboration and reduces duplicate work.** Multiple departments may already be actively learning from customers. By working together, silos are broken and there's less chance of redundancies.

Of course, you'll only enjoy these benefits if you can get everyone on board.

GETTING BUY-IN FROM PEOPLE WHO DON'T WANT TO BUY IN

Resistance to this work typically shows up in one of two forms: resistance to investing time in customer research or to the idea of forming a cross-functional team of very busy people. If your team members raise any objections, here are some ways to address them.

RESISTANCE TO CUSTOMER RESEARCH

When teams are deciding whether to invest time and energy into customer research, we see two common concerns:

- "What if all this does is slow us down?"
- "What if we end up even more confused than we are now?"

Customer research may sound daunting or time consuming, but here's the thing: *you can't afford **not** to take this time.*

Your team implementing inefficient, ineffective tactics is *already* wasting time. If you don't act now, your team will continue wasting time, effort, and resources. They'll continue to burn out or even quit. Chaos will continue to reign.

As for being even more confused than you are now, the process outlined in Part II nips this issue in the bud. We'll walk you step-by-step through segmenting the customers you'll learn from, identifying what to ask them, and then how to extract what matters. By the end of this process, **you'll know exactly what to do with what you learn.**

RESISTANCE TO FORMING A CROSS-FUNCTIONAL TEAM

Skepticism about cross-functional teams is valid. When not managed properly, they can quickly become dysfunctional and waste time. In fact, a *Harvard Business Review* study found that 75% of all cross-functional teams fail in at least three of the five criteria for functionality:[1]

1. Meeting a planned budget
2. Staying on schedule
3. Adhering to specifications
4. Meeting customer expectations
5. Maintaining alignment with the company's larger goals

Take note, though: **this happens when the team lacks a systematic approach.** Lack of clear ownership, vague or nonexistent goals, and/or lack of specificity is what creates dysfunction.

---

1 Behnam Tabrizi, "75% of Cross-Functional Teams are Dysfunctional," *Harvard Business Review*, June 23, 2015, https://hbr.org/2015/06/75-of-cross-functional-teams-are-dysfunctional.

But you have the Customer-Led Growth Framework—you're golden. This framework will give *your* cross-functional team (your "CLG Team") an approach to follow and specificity on what they're doing and why they're doing it. Keeping them accountable for moving forward, of course, will be up to you.

CLG TEAM ROLES AND RESPONSIBILITIES

In general, your CLG Team should consist of a Champion, a Primary Stakeholder, and key contributors.

Primary Stakeholder: Generally, this is the person with the highest decision-making power on the team (e.g., founder, CEO, COO). They're interested in the big-picture strategy. They get the team on board and excited. They're also most likely the first reader of this book (hi!).

Champion: Usually someone leading a customer-facing department (Marketing, Product, Product Marketing, or Customer Success). They have a big-picture view of the customer experience. They're able to put themselves in others' shoes (high empathy). They're the most likely to move the actions of this book forward. They might have read this book before or after the Primary Stakeholder (hello to you, too!).

Contributors/Secondary Stakeholders: These are leaders who have a stake in the outcomes of the work (e.g., Head of Product, Head of Sales, Head of Marketing, Head of Customer Service or Customer Success). They're valued and respected company-wide. They have deep expertise on different aspects of the company/product/customer. They also have the influence to guide their own departments in this new customer-led direction. They serve as *contributors* because of bandwidth, niche knowledge, personality, or desire.

Facilitator (optional): You may opt for an internal or external advisor or consultant to guide the process forward (we're often in this role). While they won't do the day-to-day work, they will steer the ship, which speeds things up and relieves the Champion of having to play project manager and have all the answers.

These roles can generally be mapped onto the ones recommended in the popular role assignment matrix RACI, which stands for *responsible, accountable, consulted, informed*:

- The Champion is the person **responsible** for getting things done.
- The Primary Stakeholder is the person **accountable** for making sure the Champion is unblocked and the overall project is a success.
- The Secondary Stakeholders/Contributors are **consulted**, playing a part on the team but not driving the work.

RACI also includes people who are **informed**. They're the folks who are aware of the work and who should be kept in the loop, but whose input or contribution isn't required (i.e., the CTO/COO/less involved founders).

Of course, nothing falls apart if you don't have someone for each of these roles. Just adapt and go with who you have.

The following role worksheets give you a snapshot view of each of the key roles:

ROLE	CHAMPION (RESPONSIBLE)
Description	• Person in a leading role in a customer-facing department • Has a big-picture view of the customer experience; can see details and options that others don't • Already doing this kind of work in a less formalized way, or inherently understands the value of being customer focused • Able to put themselves in others' shoes (high empathy) • Moves the actions of this book forward; might have read it before or after the Primary Stakeholder
Time investment	Heavy time commitment; will need to take the work on as a special project, but we've streamlined the process to save them *serious* time
Actions	• Calls and runs the meetings • Drives the work forward • Keeps everyone accountable

ROLE	PRIMARY STAKEHOLDER (ACCOUNTABLE)
Description	• Person with highest level of decision-making power on the team (e.g., founder, CEO, COO) • Main contact for the Facilitator and Champion • Gets exec buy-in, removes roadblocks • Interested in big-picture strategy • Gets team on board and excited about customer-led growth • Most likely the first reader of this book
Time investment	Highest at the beginning; low once the project kicks off
Actions	• Sends kickoff email and leads kickoff meeting • Facilitates team role selection • Passes baton to chosen Champion • Cheerleads and unblocks work as needed

ROLE	CONTRIBUTORS/SECONDARY STAKEHOLDERS (CONSULTED)
Description	• Leaders who have a stake in the outcomes of the work • Valued and respected by Primary Stakeholder • Have insights and knowledge of customer facing work • Have deep expertise on different aspects of the company/product/customer • Have influence to guide their own department teams in this new customer-led direction • Serve as contributors because of bandwidth, niche knowledge, personality, or desire
Time investment	Minimal and as needed
Actions	• Participate and contribute in meetings • Provide timely input • Review work, give feedback

WILL IT WORK FOR YOU?

Customer-Led Growth has worked for companies at many different stages of growth and with various combinations of participants. Here are some examples:

- Tiller Money: 6 employees. Team led by Gia as the facilitator/advisor. Team: Head of Customer Success, Head of Marketing, Founder and CEO, and CTO.
- Unbounce: 25 employees. Team: Director of Marketing (Gia), Co-founder and Head of Product, and Director of Customer Success.
- Sprout Social: 200 employees. Team: Director of Marketing Strategy, Growth Director, UX (user experience) Design Director. (Note: They held regular workshops with company leaders and key stakeholders because the company was big enough that they couldn't involve them all directly.)

TOOLS TO HELP KICK OFF THE PROJECT

With your team in mind, it's time to push this project forward and get everyone aligned. We've built some resources to help you get buy-in and get things started:

1. Role worksheets so that everyone is clear on what is needed from them
2. A project brief to capture and communicate your goals
3. A kickoff email to get everyone on board
4. A kickoff meeting agenda to get everyone aligned

You can grab those templates in the workbook.

CALMING THE CHAOS STARTS HERE

Remember Tara's work at Sprout Social? The primary reason her customer-led efforts were successful is because she had buy-in at every level. Everyone on the team, from the top exec to the regular contributors, saw how being customer-led could help both the marketing department and the company as a whole. As a result, they were willing to invest time and resources up front so they could calm the chaos, create the clarity needed, and ultimately increase revenue.

If you are the Primary Stakeholder, as the driver of this mindset shift and framework adoption, you have to protect the process. Nothing happens—from team formation, to buy-in, to action—without you.

To gain customer insight, the Champion will lead the process of running customer research and deciding what existing collective knowledge (past research, internal subject matter expertise, etc.) to use.

That's when the real work of getting inside your ideal customer's head starts. We'll walk you through the process of uncovering those insights in the next chapter.

YOUR TURN

Your biggest responsibilities as Primary Stakeholder are putting the team on the starting line and shouting, "Go!" Here's a shortlist of how to do that:

1. Draft a short project brief so everyone knows the direction you're headed in and why.
2. Choose who's on your team and what roles they'll play.
3. Send an email to get everyone scheduled for the kickoff meeting.
4. Hold your kickoff meeting.

Grab tools to help at forgetthefunnel.com/workbook.

Part II

GETTING INSIDE YOUR CUSTOMERS' HEADS

Chapter 3

LEARNING FROM CUSTOMERS

The team at Autobooks had a great product: an all-in-one finance management platform for small business owners.

They had a solid channel for acquiring new customers: partnering with banks and credit unions, who then worked *with* Autobooks to spread the word to the banks' small business customers. Their finance management features were *right there* when a small business owner logged into their bank account.

Valuable product and solid acquisition channel in place, it was time to invest heavily in landing more new customers. So Chris Spiek, Autobooks's VP of Customer Acquisition at the time (and prior to Autobooks, one of the pioneers of the Jobs-to-be-Done theory), led the team in running interviews with their most engaged customers: those who were using the product frequently and loved it.

Out of those interviews came something surprising.

Up to that point, Autobooks had emphasized that the platform was an "all-in-one": invoicing, bill pay, bookkeeping, accounting, and so much other good stuff. But the research showed that only *one* feature set actually got small business owners through the door: online invoicing and payment processing.

Because the team understood internally how powerful the all-in-one platform was, their messaging had been throwing all of Autobooks's features at customers all at once. But that's like throwing a whole toolbox at someone who just needs a wrench.

Customers didn't *understand* and didn't have *time* to sort out an all-in-one finance management platform. And that was Autobooks's key takeaway: they needed to narrow down their messaging and highlight the *one* feature that made their customers' lives easier.

Everything about how they talked to small businesses needed reworking.

* * *

They brought Claire in to lead the messaging overhaul: "Give your customers a way to pay you by credit card, right into your bank account." That most-desired feature became the *only* thing the new messaging highlighted; it clarified for new customers that *yes*, this is the wrench you've been looking for.

Once customers grew more confident, *then* Autobooks

could introduce its additional features—or more accurately, introduce *one* more tool at a time, in a way that addressed customers' next most pressing need.

The team went from focusing on customers' *presumed* pain to their *real* pain. They went from *believing* which features created value for customers, to *knowing* which features created value. This allowed them to plan which features to introduce second, third, fourth, and beyond. They could leverage their invoicing and payment processing as a gateway feature to the rest of their suite of features. **Marketing became more of a curated, coursed meal than a super buffet.**

And it worked. Thirty days after this overhaul—changing the customer experience to match customers' actual needs— the team saw a 64% increase in the rate of small business owners signing up for Autobooks after first learning about it (from 14% to 23%). What's more, they saw a 300% increase in the number of customers accepting credit card payments through their platform on a sustained basis. And given that processing payments is how Autobooks generates revenue, these were pretty exciting outcomes.

Uncovering insights through customer research gave Autobooks the real answers to their growth problem. If they hadn't done research, they'd still be throwing solutions at the wrong problem.

WHY YOU NEED *NEW* CUSTOMER RESEARCH

You may be thinking, "Been there, done that. We did tons of

research when we developed our product." It's a common pushback, and we get it: of course you've already done customer research. A product can't be built out of nothing.

Or we hear "We already know our customers because we *are* our customers." It's super common for a product to be created by someone who once had their own "I can't take it anymore" day, didn't find what they needed, and decided to build a solution.

But building a product in the first place is one thing. Learning from customers' experience actually *using* it is another. As your company innovates, as your team grows, your product evolves. Your customers change, too. Their needs shift as old problems are solved, as industries mature, and as more solutions enter the market.

Another problem with relying on past research is that it often gives you answers to the *wrong* questions. It may have focused on demographics—age, location, gender, job titles, etc.—but demographics can't tell you customers' struggles or desired outcomes. Or it may have focused on product usage, telling you which parts of your product customers are and aren't using, do or don't want—but not telling you *why.* **Neither demographic data nor product data tell you what's inside customers' heads.**

Instead, you want to create a documentary of your best customer's journey: from the struggle, to the search for solutions, to finding your product, to trying it, to buying it and being so happy that someone would now have to pry it from their hands.

If you haven't done the kind of customer research that can tell you *that*, and you have a marketing or growth problem, you need new research. (More on how often to *repeat* your research in Chapter 9.)

HOW TO CAPTURE CUSTOMER INSIGHTS

So *how* do you capture those insights? How do you get inside your best customers' heads and understand the journey they've taken from struggle to whole-hearted adoption?

In the simplest terms, you ask questions, gather answers, and analyze what you find.

In the next section, you'll find a quick overview of tried-and-true methods for finding the customers who'd be *happy* to talk to you.

When you and your CLG Team are ready to dig in and do the work, you can find a bunch more in-depth, *how-to* resources and best practices in the workbook.

IDENTIFY YOUR BEST CUSTOMERS

Not all customers are created equal. You want to learn from your best, your "pry it from my hands" customers who:

- understand the problem your product solves and have personally struggled with it;
- pay for the value your product provides without hesitation;

- have an ongoing need for your product (not a one-off use case);
- have reached what we call "value realization"—they've clearly solved the problem they wanted to solve using your product; and
- began paying recently enough that they remember what life was like before they found your product (ideally three to six months ago; up to a year ago for some products).

These are the customers you want to learn from, since *these* are the customers you want more of.

START ASKING QUESTIONS

Henry Ford has been famously misquoted as saying, "If I had asked my customers what they wanted, they would have said a faster horse." People often take this misquote to heart and assume talking to customers is a waste of time. Customers aren't product experts, after all.

But talking to customers is only a problem if you take what they say at *face value*, rather than looking for the underlying psychology—the pains and needs behind their actions and desires (we'll dig into how to do this in Chapter 5).

That's why understanding customers' psychology, not their opinions, is at the heart of the questions you ask.

What to Ask and How to Ask It

No matter what format you use to gather customer data (interviews, surveys, etc.), the goal is the same: build a storyboard of customers' *real,* step-by-step experience, from life before they ever knew they needed your product to the ongoing value and growth they're now enjoying.

Getting good, usable data around this goal relies entirely on **how you word your questions.** You want to avoid inviting opinions or speculation and avoid leading or closed questions. Try to gain an understanding of *what happened* that pushed your customer to seek new solutions, then what happened next and next and next.

Keep in mind, too, that open-ended questions are the only way to gather the *real words and phrases* your customers naturally use to describe their struggles, motivations, and desired outcomes. Multiple choice and true/false questions force your customers to choose from a set of answers and phrasing you've *assumed* about their experience.

LEADING/CLOSED QUESTIONS (BAD)	OPEN-ENDED QUESTIONS (GOOD)
Are you happy with your experience so far?	How would you describe your experience so far?
Which competitors have you tried?	How have you tried to solve this problem in the past?
Which is your favorite feature: A, B, C or D?	When you first tried our product, what was it that convinced you it would solve your problem?

Open-ended questions like these give you rich insight into not only the customer's experience, but also the customer's voice, which—*bonus*—guides the words you should use in your marketing and overall messaging.

Now that you know *how* to ask, here's *what* we ask:

- How are you using [product name] day-to-day?
- When did you first start using [product name]?
- Okay, so with that timeline in mind, take me back to life before [product name]. Prior to [product name], what were you using instead? If you were using a combination of any tools or products, what were those?
- Tell me about the moment you realized [old way] wasn't cutting it. What caused that moment? What compelled you to look for something different?
- Where did you go to look for new solutions? Did you try anything else before [product name]?
- How did you find out about [product name]?
- Why did you decide to choose [product name] over other options? Can you recall anything that stood out to you?
- When you signed up for [product name], what happened that made you feel certain it was the right solution for you?
- Now that you have [product name], what's the number one thing you're able to do that you weren't able to do before?
- What do you wish [product name] did that it doesn't do today?

You can grab a copy of these questions in the workbook.

Notice that these questions ask customers to report on *what happened:* the situation that led them to be dissatisfied with their old solution, actions they took, and specific details about the product that stood out to them.

Now let's walk through what format you'll use to reach your customers.

Surveys vs. Interviews

You can ask your customers these questions by sending them a survey, or by holding one-on-one interviews. Here's how to identify which methods are right for you.

Surveys

If your pool of ideal customers is 500 people or more, start with a survey. Betting on an average survey response rate of between 10–15%, sending it to 500 happy customers will give you enough responses to feel confidence in the data you gather. Surveys can quickly give you a broad view of your ideal customers, help you tee up interviews, and can validate patterns in data gathered through other research methods.

As great as surveys are for quickly learning from a larger number of customers, though, they won't give you nuanced details. They don't humanize or describe. For that, you need interviews.

Interviews

If you have fewer than 500 people in your best customer pool—or if you have time and resources for only *one* research method—choose interviews. Interviews give you an opportunity to clarify and get data beyond just words. In interviews, you can feel the energy, hear the verbal cues and emotion, even pick up on body language if you're using video. Interviews provide a much richer understanding of your customer's story.

NUMBER OF IDEAL CUSTOMERS	METHOD	TARGET NUMBER OF PARTICIPANTS
500 or fewer	Interviews	10–15 interviewees
More than 500	Surveys and/or interviews	25–50 survey respondents with high-quality responses

We cover how to run successful surveys and interviews in the workbook.

GETTING CUSTOMERS

Through customer research, Autobooks could finally understand the struggle that pushed their ideal customers to look for something new: they weren't getting paid quickly enough.

Once the Autobooks team understood this, they were able to get so much smarter about the way they described their product and how it could help. They could hide all of the extra bells and whistles at first, so the small business owner could quickly find the "get paid" feature and not feel overwhelmed by everything else.

Once customers got paid the first time, Autobooks could send more relevant point-of-need communication: "Hey, you got paid, congrats! Did you know there are three other ways Autobooks can make your life easier?" and so on.

These customer insights not only solved Autobooks's initial problem of not acquiring new customers; they also enabled Autobooks to retain those customers longer term and increase their engagement with the platform over time.

In a sense, your documentary of "How I Met Your Product" is really a documentary about how your customer fell in love with your product. Your findings will tell you how to be a better matchmaker in the future.

But before we get into how to parse and apply these findings (in Chapter 5), in the *next* chapter, we'll talk about another group of people to learn from: your *future* customers.

YOUR TURN

If you haven't chosen a Champion yet, you'll need to do that now. Here are your Champion's first action items:

1. Identify your best customers.
2. Decide whether you'll use interviews, surveys, or both.
3. Get the research resources from our website: outreach email template, interview script template, survey template, etc.
4. If running a survey, build your survey using the tools of your choice.
5. Reach out to your best customers, inviting them to complete your survey and/or schedule interviews.
6. Run your survey and/or interviews!

Grab those customer research resources at forgetthefunnel. com/workbook.

Chapter 4

LEARNING FROM FUTURE CUSTOMERS

We started working with the team at Paytouch in February 2020. Their all-in-one restaurant management platform handled point-of-sale (i.e., processing customers' payments), plus back-of-house operations including product inventory, employee management, analytics, and more. Basically, *the works.*

Given what a robust platform it was, the onboarding process to get new restaurants up and running on Paytouch was long and labor intensive. Our goal in working together was to simplify new customer onboarding, which would shorten restaurants' time to value and lower the burden on their customer support team.

Then the COVID-19 pandemic hit.

Shutdowns ensued across the US (and the globe), and restaurants were forced into survival mode. *No one* was in the market for an all-in-one restaurant management platform. Growth screeched to a halt. In a blink, our goal went from "make onboarding easier" to "get through a pandemic." We had to face reality: Paytouch *would not* sell as is. We needed to quickly understand the new, urgent problems restaurants were facing and shift gears.

Prior to the pandemic, we'd done some research with Paytouch's original customer base. As a result, we knew that one of restaurants' biggest pain points was managing all of the different delivery services customers used to place to-go orders: DoorDash, Postmates, Uber Eats, etc. That pain only got worse with COVID-19, when to-go orders suddenly became the *only* thing restaurants could offer.

Within the Paytouch platform, it was relatively easy to set up an online menu and ordering system—an offering that could prove especially valuable to restaurants that, prior to COVID-19, didn't have any kind of online menu or ordering system set up. The team hadn't previously targeted these "offline" restaurants—but in the context of the pandemic, *they* were the customers who stood to benefit most from the product's online menu and ordering features.

What if Paytouch repackaged this set of features as a separate, smaller product? Could the business stay afloat this way, helping offline restaurants transition to accepting online orders and deliveries until larger restaurant groups *were* back in the market for their original product?

Unfortunately, there was no way to validate this idea through customer research, since Paytouch didn't have any offline restaurants as customers. It was time to turn to the next best thing: **audience research.** We studied what these restaurant owners were doing out in the real world—the conversations they were having in forums and communities; the ways they described their pain points and needs; the other solutions they were trying, and why those solutions didn't work for them. We worked with Paytouch to develop positioning and messaging for this new product called Dash, as well as a launch plan to evaluate whether there really *was* demand for a solution like it.

It worked. Hundreds of restaurants began signing up, desperate to begin accepting online orders. And with customers to learn from, the team could start iterating on the product's messaging, signup flow, onboarding experience, etc., tailoring Dash to the most urgent needs of these transitioning restaurants.

Ultimately, **980 restaurants became Dash customers—** restaurants that otherwise wouldn't have been aware of (or in the market for) Paytouch at all. And as restaurants reopened their doors and patrons returned to dining in, **Dash customers with multiple restaurant locations ended up converting into full-fledged Paytouch customers.**

Customer research is your best tool to drive customer-led growth—when you have customers to get insight from. When you're launching a new product, or suddenly need to pivot, like Paytouch, or when you don't yet have enough pry-it-from-my-hands customers, *audience* research is your ticket.

AUDIENCE RESEARCH

Audience research is learning from your target audience or potential customers out in the world experiencing the problem that you help solve.

Audience research helps you understand:

- what influences the people you're trying to reach;
- who they listen to and trust;
- where they go when they're looking for new solutions; and
- other solutions they're trying, and why those solutions are/aren't working for them.

Capturing audience insights is similar to capturing customer insights: you're not looking for user experience or demographic data. You're looking for people's objective, observable actions and answers. You're looking for information about the problem they're trying to solve, the places they look for solutions, and the tactics they use to track down solutions.

Keep in mind, though: not everyone in your audience, out in the wild, is automatically an ideal customer. When learning from your current, happy customers, you know for a fact that they're a fit. When learning from your target audience, you can't know that for sure. This just means the results will be more *hypotheses you'll want to prove or disprove*, rather than a path you're *certain* you should take.

Even so, audience insights are still incredibly valuable. They give you a directional understanding of your target customers so your team doesn't have to take wild guesses.

There are many ways to collect audience insights. You can:

- Run target market interviews
- Send a survey to your email subscribers
- Mine reviews of competing solutions
- Use audience intelligence or customer discovery tools
- Do social listening in forums and communities where your target audience hangs out

We've pulled together some of our favorite audience research tools and resources for you in the workbook.

For Dash, exploring forums, communities, and review sites was the only path forward, but these options can take practice and are often labor intensive. If, unlike Dash, you already have a product and a website, then **a website survey is your quickest, most straightforward way to get the info you need.**

WEBSITE SURVEYS

If you've already invested in sending traffic to your site—be it from ads, content marketing, social media, etc.—why spend time wading through third-party sources? Why not learn from people you already know are in problem-solving mode?

RESPONDENTS

Asking your website visitors a few quick questions gives you a window into your future customers' thought process while they're *actively seeking* a solution like yours. It helps you understand how sharply they're feeling the problem your product solves, and what matters most to them as they look for ways to solve that problem.

Of course, not everyone who answers your website survey is automatically your ideal customer. It would be great if those respondents *became* your customers, but you can't know for sure who's out there perusing your website.

That's the big difference between customer and audience research: whose voice you capture. **In customer research, you start with the narrowest band of *quality*, the cream of the crop. With audience research, you start with a wider band of *quantity*.** You might get some junk responses (that's normal), but the good responses you get will be worth it.

WEBSITE SURVEY QUESTIONS

The goal of your website survey is to document your *potential* customer's life before they've found a solution. Here are the questions to ask:

1. Which of these best describes you?
   A. I'm considering a [product type] for the first time; not sure it's for me yet.
   B. I know I need a [product type]. I'm just trying to find the best option.
   C. I know [product name], but I'm not a customer yet.
   D. I'm already using [product name]. I'm just here to sign in.
   E. Other [click to type].
2. What tool(s) do you currently use for [problem], if anything? (online or offline)

3. Is there anything you dislike or want to change about your current solution(s)? If so, please describe.
4. What matters **most** as you look for a new solution?
5. Is there anything holding you back from [booking a demo/signing up] right now?

The wording of these questions is intentional. Here's what you'll learn from each one.

The multiple-choice first question—**Which of these best describes you?**—helps you understand the level of awareness most of your visitors are at when they arrive on your site: how aware of your *product* they are, of the *problem* you solve, and how ready they are to *take action.*

The second question—**What tool(s) do you currently use for [problem], if anything?**—provides insight on what visitors currently use to solve their problem. If they're not using anything, it gives details as to what life is like before your product.

The third question—**Is there anything you dislike or want to change about your current solution(s)?**—reveals how their current solution contributes to their struggle. It highlights what's not working.

The fourth question—**What matters most as you look for a new solution?**—is especially important: it uncovers what message to prioritize on your website. It enables you to say: "Hey, we know you struggle with X! Guess what: we have your solution!"

The fifth question—**Is there anything holding you back**

from [booking a demo/signing up] right now?—helps you understand the anxieties, unanswered questions, and other blockers that prevent your website visitors from taking action.

Now, you might be concerned about how a website survey could impact your conversion rates. Or maybe you're worried about distracting visitors who may otherwise be qualified leads. Don't worry; we have best practices and specific advice on how to run a survey that takes these concerns into account.

Just like with our customer research resources, you can grab a copy of these website survey questions and our survey best practices in the workbook.

Solution-Seekers to Solution-Getters

When Gia began working with Tiller Money (a personal finance tool), the company already had a happy, loyal customer base. The team was looking for opportunities to get to the next level of growth. Gia worked with them to launch a website survey, using the same questions described earlier.

Through that website survey, the team uncovered:

- website visitors' most common pain points, current solutions, and requirements as they looked for something new;
- the *actual words and phrases* they use; and
- the order in which to arrange messages and information on the site, according to their priorities

With this insight, they reorganized and rewrote the homepage, leveraging sticky copy straight from survey responses. The results of this simple survey and subsequent actions from it? **The page value in Google Analytics increased 237%.**

For Tiller Money, audience research gave them an additional level of insight to their customer research. In looking to their *potential* customers, they learned how to expand the appeal of their already appealing product. They broadened their customer base, bringing more customers into the fold. Solution-seekers became solution-getters. Win-win.

FROM DATA TO "AHA"

So let's fast-forward in time, to the point at which *your* CLG Team has done the research. You've run your surveys and interviews. You've got data in hand. Now what?

Now it's time to *parse* that data. Parsing—which we'll cover next—is how you'll find the patterns that lead to game-changing "aha" moments for your team and make your biggest opportunities for growth so much more obvious.

YOUR TURN

Depending on your situation, you may want to use more than one of the audience research methods we've talked about here. No matter what, though, if a website survey is an option for you, we recommend not waiting to launch it. Depending on the amount of traffic coming to your site, it can take a few weeks for enough quality responses to roll in. Why not have it work for you in the background as you make your way through this book?

1. Get the website survey questions and best practices from the workbook.
2. Build your survey and test it out to make sure it's working properly on your site.
3. Launch your survey and let responses start rolling in!

Grab those audience research resources at forgetthefunnel.com/workbook.

Chapter 5

IDENTIFYING YOUR CUSTOMERS' JOBS-TO-BE-DONE

Alistair, a marketing tool for small businesses, had grown to $2 million ARR and 5,000 customers thanks to a heavy investment in marketing. Content marketing, social media, paid advertising, partnerships—they'd leveraged it all.

But what had gotten them to their first couple million wasn't getting them to their next several. Growth had flatlined, and the company's revenue was heading toward a decline—even as their investment in marketing continued.

Thankfully, the team at Alistair decided to invest in learning more about their customers. After just a few months, **trial signups on their website increased 89% and their trial-to-paid conversion rate by 40%**. And not because they'd found some holy grail new marketing channel, but because they better understood their best customers' Jobs-to-be-Done.

CUSTOMER-LED GROWTH AND JOBS-TO-BE-DONE

When we say "Jobs-to-be-Done," what we mean is:

1. The *struggle*...
2. That *motivated* customers...
3. To seek a desired outcome.

Before a potential customer had ever heard of Alistair, a **struggle** arose that pushed them to look for a new marketing tool. They had specific **motivations** guiding their search: features or attributes they needed that their previous solution lacked. Finally, they had a **desired outcome** in mind: how life would be better once they found the perfect new solution.

The team at Alistair whittled their 5,000 customers down to just 500 of their healthiest, happiest customers (covered in Chapter 3), and then identified two distinct Jobs that brought customers to their product (we'll dive into *how* they did it later in this chapter):

1. **The need to increase their marketing presence.** For customers with this Job, the *struggle* was that business was slower than they'd like. Not enough people were visiting their websites, so they were looking to ramp up their marketing.
2. **The need to save time and automate.** For customers with this Job, the *struggle* was completely different. Business was humming along, marketing was working...but it had all become too time-consuming to manage.

Understanding these two Jobs changed everything. The differences between a small business just getting started with marketing and a business that already understands the value of marketing were significant.

For the "just getting started" folks (let's call them "Newbies"), there's *so* much to learn. There's no guarantee that the marketing channel they've picked will work, no guarantee that spending time on it will pay off.

In contrast, businesses that have already figured out their marketing (let's call them "Pros") know which marketing channels work for them. They're okay with investing time and resources because they've seen it pay off. Now they just need to automate low-level tasks—and if Alistair can automate marketing tasks for them, they're likely to stick around.

With this new level of clarity, the team knew Pros represented the better opportunity. But when they looked at their messaging, content marketing, ads, etc., they realized they'd been trying to sell to both Pros *and* Newbies. And worse, some of their biggest investments were designed *specifically* to attract Newbies.

The team rewrote their homepage, features page, and pricing page, focusing on what a time-saver the product was and highlighting specific features their Pro customers loved. The result: **trial signups increased by 89%**.

And because their new messaging attracted more advanced, marketing-savvy businesses, those businesses had an easier time *learning how to use* Alistair. As a result, the changes on Alistair's website led to a **40% increase in trial-to-paid conversions**, too.

Now, let's talk about *how* Alistair identified their customers' Jobs, so you can do the same.

HOW TO FIND CUSTOMERS' JOBS-TO-BE-DONE

To understand the Job your customer "hires" your solution for—the one that led them to "fire" their past solution, search for new ones, and ultimately choose yours—you need clarity on:

- The *struggle*... (When I...)
- That *motivated* customers...(help me...)
- To seek a *desired outcome* (so I can...).

Taken together, these three elements (struggle, motivation, desired outcome) summarize your customer's experience into a **customer *job statement*** (Figure 5.1).

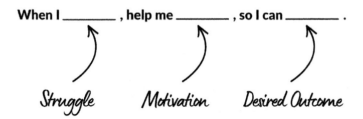

Figure 5.1. The structure of a customer job statement

The customer job statement for Alistair's Pro customers was:

- ***When I*** need a way to automate my marketing content... (struggle)
- ***Help me*** manage it all in a way that's simple but still helps me be strategic...(motivation)

- *So I can* feel more confident and organized (desired outcome).

To fill in the blanks for *your* customer, we'll look to the data gathered from your customer and audience research.

The four steps we'll take are:

1. Identify the struggles, motivations, and desired outcomes in the responses to your questions
2. Look for the common themes
3. Define the top few Jobs your customers hire your solution for
4. Pick one Job to prioritize

Let's dig in.

STEP 1: IDENTIFY STRUGGLES, MOTIVATIONS, AND DESIRED OUTCOMES

To start things off, we'll connect the dots between specific interview/survey questions and the blanks their answers fill. To do this, we'll look for language that sounds like your customer is describing their struggle, their motivations, and their desired outcomes. Then we'll summarize them with a theme.

When you're ready, you can grab the database template we've built for you in the workbook. For now though, don't worry too much about the mechanics.

Struggle

To identify your customers' struggles, you're going to look for instances where your customer talks about the pain they experienced that pushed them to start looking for a new solution. Struggles might show up as actual *problems* your customer felt, or *situations* that triggered a need.

Customers' struggles will appear in response to these kinds of questions:

- Take me back to life before [product name]. Prior to [product name], what were you using instead? If you were using a combination of any tools or products, what were those?
- Tell me about the moment you realized [old way] wasn't cutting it. What caused that moment? What compelled you to look for something different?
- Where did you go to look for new solutions? Did you try anything else before [product name]?

Here's an example from one of Alistair's customer survey responses: *"I was struggling to post on social media every day, on top of doing all of the other business things! Engagement was really low, and my community wasn't hearing from me enough."*

Next, as you're reading through responses, you'll notice that each can be summarized into a *theme*—the main idea of what the customer is saying. As you read more responses, you'll see more themes. Here are some example answers from Alistair's customers to show what we mean:

	SURVEY RESPONSE	STRUGGLE THEME
Customer A	*"I was struggling to post on social media every day, on top of doing all of the other business things! Engagement was really low, and my community wasn't hearing from me enough."*	Increase marketing presence
Customer B	*"I wanted to reuse the content I was working so hard on."*	Reuse content
Customer C	*"I needed more automation, I am a very busy person."*	Save time and automate

For each response in your research, you'll make a note of the theme and continue on to the next customer. It's okay if there are two or three themes within one quote—that's totally normal. Go ahead and note them all down.

It's easier to go through all the responses related to struggle, noting all struggle themes as you go, before moving on to motivations.

For now though, let's keep going.

Motivation

Now let's look for what *motivated* your customers. Motivations are the specifics of a new solution **that fill the gaps** customers' old solutions couldn't fill. They're the specific *attributes* of your solution that enable your customer to solve their problem.

Customers' motivations will appear in response to these kinds of questions:

- What was the most important to you in a new solution?
- Why did you decide to choose us over the other options? Can you recall if anything in particular stood out to you?
- What deal breakers would have prevented you from choosing us?
- Once you started using our product, what happened that made you feel certain it was right for you?

Again, for each response, make a note of the theme and continue on to the next customer. There might be two or three themes within one quote—go ahead and note them all down. Here are some example answers from Alistair's customers:

	SURVEY RESPONSE	MOTIVATION THEME(S)
Customer A	*"I liked that Alistair picks the best times for my content to go live."*	Done for me Strategic
Customer B	*"I could finally post all my content in a strategic, goal-oriented way."*	Strategic
Customer C	*"The training was easy to access and set me up to start using it right away"*	Easy setup

Just like with struggle themes, it's easiest if you finish identifying all the motivation themes for all your customer responses before moving on.

Desired Outcome

Time to rinse and repeat once more—this time, looking for customers' *desired outcomes.*

Your customer's desired outcome is the picture they have in their head of *how life will be better* once they've found a solution that fits their motivations.

Customers' desired outcome themes will appear in response to these questions:

- How are you using [product name] day-to-day?
- What's the number one thing you're able to do now, that you weren't able to do before?

As with struggle and motivation, you might identify more than one theme for each answer. Go ahead and write them all down. Here are some example answers from Alistair's customers:

	SURVEY RESPONSE	DESIRED OUTCOME THEME(S)
Customer A	*"Post all my marketing content in a strategic, organized way."*	Strategic and organized
Customer B	*"I feel confident that my content is going live at the right times, without me having to post manually."*	Confident
Customer C	*"I have time to do the things that are really important in my business."*	Time better spent

Customer	Struggle Response	Struggle Theme	Motivation Response	Motivation Theme	Desired Outcome Response	Desired Outcome Theme
A	"I was struggling to post on social media every day, on top of doing all of the other business things! Engagement was really low, and my community wasn't hearing from me enough."	Increase marketing presence	"I liked that Alistair picks the best times for my content to go live."	Done for me / Strategic	"Post all my marketing content in a strategic, organized way."	Strategic and organized
B	"I wanted to reuse the content I was working so hard on."	Reuse content	"I could finally post all my content in a strategic, goal-oriented way."	Strategic	"I feel confident that my content is going live at the right times, without me having to post manually."	Confident
C	"I needed more automation. I am a very busy person."	Save time and automate	"The training was easy to access and set me up to start using it right away."	Easy setup	"I have time to do the things that are really important in my business."	Time better spent
D	"We knew we needed to get a lot more content out there to grow."	Increase marketing presence	"The customer service I received."	Customer support	"I can clearly see the analytics of my content."	Understand performance
E	"Manually posting was becoming stressful. I needed something faster."	Save time and automate	"Don't have to post manually anymore."	Done for me	"I feel secure that my content will post at the best times and on schedule."	Strategic and organized

Figure 5.2. Database with themes identified for struggle, motivation, and desired outcome responses

To help you visualize the responses and themes for three sections in one place, you'll use a spreadsheet or database that allows you to add tags and create charts (there's a template for you in the workbook). In Figure 5.2, you can see the various *themes* that appeared in Alistair's customer responses.

STEP 2: LOOK FOR THE MOST COMMON THEMES

After you connect themes to all three parts of the job statement, you'll shift focus back to just the struggle themes. You now want to know which struggles appear *most often* across *your* customer data.

Once all of Alistair's customer struggle themes were identified, pulling them into a chart (Figure 5.3) made it clear which struggles were *most common.*

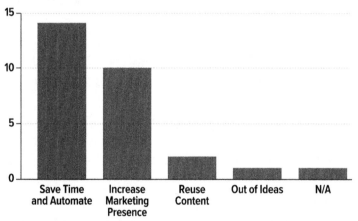

Figure 5.3. Alistair customers' struggle themes

The number one most common struggle for Alistair's customers: *save time and automate.* Their second most common struggle: *increase marketing presence.*

With your customers' top struggles identified, you'll be ready to start drafting a few customer job statements.

STEP 3: DEFINE CUSTOMERS' TOP JOBS-TO-BE-DONE

As a quick reminder, customer job statements are typically written in three parts:

- When...*struggle*
- Help me...*motivation*
- So I can...*desired outcome.*

Crafting your customer job statements means taking the top struggle themes (from the previous step) and **identifying the motivations and desired outcomes *connected to* each top struggle theme.** Starting with the most common struggle. Let's say it's the same as Alistair's: *save time and automate.* Here's how it works:

1. First, you'll identify the customers who expressed this "save time and automate" struggle, and filter out the rest of your customers for now.
2. Then, you'll look at the motivations voiced by the customers who expressed the struggle "save time and automate." Which motivation themes are the most common among those customers?
3. Next, you'll look at the desired outcomes voiced by the customers who expressed the struggle "save time and automate." Which desired outcome themes are the most common among those customers?
4. Fitting those three pieces—the associated struggle, moti-

vation, and desired outcome—you'll have the beginnings of your customer job statement. For example:

A. When I need a way to save time and automate my marketing content...(struggle)
B. Help me manage it in a way that's simple to set up and that's done for me...(motivation)
C. So I can spend my time more effectively (desired outcome).

Figure 5.4 shows how customers' top struggle, plus their connected motivations and desired outcomes, came together for Alistair.

Repeat steps 1–4 for the second most common struggle theme, and then for the third most common if one exists.

Even if they're rough, you'll have two to three customer job statements summarizing the top reasons your ideal customers seek out a solution like yours—and, ultimately, why they fall in love with your product in each scenario.

Just like parsing customer data, crafting job statements takes practice. There are guides in the workbook to help.

With your ideal customers' top Jobs defined, you know what happened in those customers' lives that made them realize, "This isn't working. I can't live like this anymore." **This is a big deal.**

Customer	Struggle Response	Struggle Theme	Motivation Response	Motivation Theme	Desired Outcome Response	Desired Outcome Theme
C	*"I needed more automation. I am a very busy person."*	**Save time and automate**	*"The training was easy to access and set me up to start using it right away."*	**Easy setup**	*"I have time to do the things that are really important in my business."*	**Time better spent**
E	*"Manually posting was becoming stressful. I needed something faster."*	**Save time and automate**	*"Don't have to post manually anymore."*	**Done for me**	*"I feel confident that my content is going live at the right times, without me having to post manually."*	**Strategic and organized**
H	*"I heard about it on a podcast. I am very busy and marketing is taking up my time."*	**Save time and automate**	*"Getting automatic notifications confirming when my posts were going live."*	**Done for me**	*"I feel secure that my content will post at the best times and on schedule."*	**Time better spent**
K	*"I was looking for ways to automate low-value tasks."*	**Save time and automate**	*"I set it up in five minutes."*	**Easy setup**	*"I don't have to worry about scheduling posts."*	**Time better spent**

Figure 5.4. Alistair customers' top motivations and desired outcomes for the "save time and automate" struggle

You can now pinpoint:

- what their previous solution looked like and why it failed them;
- where and how they look for new solutions;
- what makes your product the best choice for their needs; and
- how to match your product to their problem.

Before we get to all of that though, you'll narrow down and choose *one* customer Job.

STEP 4: PICK ONE JOB

One of the biggest mistakes we see companies make at this stage is trying to solve all of their customers' Jobs at once. But remember, Alistair's success came from focusing on *one*. That's because each job statement can represent vastly different customer needs and priorities. **Trying to optimize for all of them at the same time puts you right back where you started: chaos.**

Solving for one Job at a time gives your team focus. And from focus comes a clearer understanding of which acquisition channels to invest in; what messaging will resonate and convert best; and what features and attributes of your product to put front and center. Once you've seen some wins from solving for your first chosen customer Job, you can shift your attention to solving for others.

Your choice might already seem obvious, but just in case, there are a few helpful factors to consider when making your choice:

Urgency to solve their struggle: From the customer's perspective, which Job were people in the biggest hurry to solve? Which one required a solution *yesterday*? It's much easier to sell a painkiller than a vitamin.

Willingness to pay for value: These customers understand the value your product provides, are prepared to pay for that value, and are most likely to have the budget to do so.

Less hand holding/sales burden: For product-led solutions, these are the customers that need less support to purchase or onboard into your product. They're able to get the value it provides without constant emails or support tickets to your team. For sales-led, there is a clear champion solving the problem, there are fewer layers of leadership to convince, they have fewer questions, or they require less training.

High retention potential: Do customers with this Job have a long-term recurring need to use the product, or is it a one-off? Those with a recurring need will stick around longer and are more likely to build an ongoing habit around using the product, meaning they're less likely to churn.

Expansion and upsell potential: How likely is it that once this customer has solved their Job with your product, other struggles will arise that they can *also* solve by using additional features or upgrading to the next pricing tier?

Congregate in ways you can target: Do customers with one Job tend to gather in ways that make it easier for you to find and connect with them more than another? Demographic data may be useful to layer in here. Customers with shared job titles, stages of growth, or industry can be easier to craft messaging and target marketing for.

Other criteria, or the wildcards: There may be criteria unique to your company that could push your Job choice in one direction or another. It could be related to your company's vision—you have a higher passion for solving one particular Job over others. You may, because of your background or experience, have an unfair advantage with one over another. You could decide to prioritize one Job based on where your product and team are today. One Job might be solvable using a self-serve, product-led approach with a lower touch (and cost) to acquire customers. Another may require a sales-led approach, needing a higher touch and leading to bigger contracts. One might leverage product foremost, the other a sales team, and your company might already be stronger in one of these areas.

Here's how Alistair worked through these criteria and decided which customer Job to target:

CRITERIA	SAVE TIME AND AUTOMATE	INCREASE MY MARKETING PRESENCE
Urgency	X	X
Willingness to pay for value	X	
Minimal hand-holding/ support/sales burden	X	
High retention/low churn	X	
Expansion/upsell potential	X	X
Congregate in ways we can target	X	X

Remember that Alistair's "increase my marketing presence" customers were the Newbies. They had *so* much to learn to be successful with the product. There was no guarantee that the marketing channel they'd picked would work, no guarantee that spending time on it would pay off.

In contrast, the "save time and automate" customers were the Pros. They knew *which* marketing channels worked for them. They were okay with investing time and resources because they'd already seen it pay off. Now, they just needed to automate low-level tasks—and if Alistair could automate marketing tasks for them, they were more likely to stick around.

Alistair's 89% trial signup increase and 40% trial-to-paid conversion increase weren't luck. Those results came from the hard work of choosing *one* customer Job to prioritize and shifting gears accordingly.

YOUR CUSTOMER'S JOB IS YOUR TICKET

With your top-priority customer Job chosen, you'll have **the most valuable guardrails money can buy.** You and your team will be able to:

- zero in on your customers' real previous solutions and why they failed, instead of trying to compete with potentially irrelevant competitors;
- understand where and how they look for new solutions— who they talk to, who or what influences them;
- cut through the noise and articulate what makes *your* product the best choice for *their* specific needs;

- understand what life looks like for them as they make a purchase decision and start using your product; and
- understand how life is uniquely better for them now that they've solved their struggle.

In short, you'll know their stories of "How I Met Your Product," and you'll be so much better at matching people with the solution your product provides.

Your customer Job is based on customer data. This is *not* guesswork. This is real information from real people who've experienced the struggle, been motivated to look for a solution, and fell in love with yours because it gave them their desired outcome.

This is the beginning of *your very own blueprint* for making repeatable, scalable growth happen. Now it's time to apply what you've learned to your relationship with your customer by *mapping* your customer experience.

YOUR TURN

To identify your customers' Jobs, you'll need to *parse* the customer data you collected in Chapters 3 and 4. This is how you'll find the patterns that lead to game-changing "aha" moments for your team and make your biggest opportunities for growth so much more obvious.

1. Analyze your customer data for struggles, motivations, outcomes.
2. Identify your customers' most common Jobs.
3. Choose your top priority customer job to focus on.

Grab the resources at forgetthefunnel.com/workbook.

Part III

MAPPING YOUR CUSTOMERS' EXPERIENCE

Chapter 6

DECONSTRUCTING THE CUSTOMER EXPERIENCE

Let's rewind to Gia's "headless chicken" days at Unbounce: she was stressed about hitting targets, working long hours, some months knocking it out of the park, others falling flat, but never really sure why.

While in San Francisco for a conference, Gia met up with Lenny Rachitsky, a friend and, at the time, a Product Manager at Airbnb. Lenny gave Gia a tour of the office, and it was there—in the product team's workspace—that **her mindset on marketing completely shifted.**

As she walked through a chaotic scene of loose papers and busy whiteboards, Gia noticed a single row of papers taped to one wall. She moved closer and realized they were illustrations representing Airbnb's ideal customer journey. Each sheet captured a milestone in their journey—the customer's touchpoints with Airbnb (and indirect experiences with their host, lodging, etc.), how they felt, and even a sense of *what value they experienced* before moving to the next milestone.

This was **nothing** like the generic, business-centric models Gia had been using for planning and measuring marketing, like buyer journey maps and pirate metrics (acquisition, activation, revenue, retention, and referral—or AARRR). Rather than focusing on business value, this customer journey **focused on *value delivered to the customer.***

Within a couple weeks, Gia, the Head of Customer Success, and the Head of Product (and co-founder) committed to mapping *their* customers' experience. They locked themselves in a room until they'd mapped their customers' unique milestones and identified a metric for each that represented the *customer* getting value.

That first customer experience (CX) map Gia and her teammates built wasn't perfect, but it worked. Two years after it had been shared and operationalized company-wide, revenue was up by 864%. The company was ranked number 14 in the Deloitte Top 50 fastest growing companies.

Help customers reach *their* goals, and you'll reach *yours*.

THE JOB OF THE JOB-TO-BE-DONE

Let's say one of your website visitors enters their credit card details to start a free trial. In a typical business-centric model, this might count as a win. But if that new trial user can't find the features they're looking for, their credit card entry is worthless. They'll churn because they didn't get the value they needed.

Generic frameworks like buyer journey maps and pirate metrics center on the *business* getting value rather than the *customer* getting value. They fall short in two specific ways:

1. **They shoehorn all customers' experiences into a generic set of stages—regardless of your product, industry, pricing model, customer, or problem being solved.** Your typical buyer journey map breaks down into three buckets: awareness, consideration, and purchase. End of story. This flattens all of the smaller steps your ideal customer *actually* goes through in their real-life experience. With this critical context lost, your team can only guess where your opportunities for growth are—not to mention the lost opportunities for recurring revenue businesses whose success only *begins* at first purchase.

2. **They incentivize your team to focus on *transactional* moments over *customer value* moments.** It's common for teams to measure their success based on metrics like "signup" or "paid." But this puts value *to the business* at the center of the story; not the customer's. Operating like this can lead to shortsighted thinking over time. This is especially risky for recurring revenue businesses who must *continually* prove their value to customers.

Identifying your ideal customer's Job gives you insight into *their* specific value moments—the moments your product delivers on its promise or exceeds their expectations. **With an understanding of the job they're hiring your product to solve, you can map their experience and *do something* to**

improve it. Streamline it, optimize it, reach more better-fit customers, and ensure that more of them reach their desired outcomes.

You've chosen your top-priority customer Job; the next step is to *deconstruct* the experience of those customers—through their eyes—into the phases that make up their experience.

THE ANATOMY OF YOUR CUSTOMER'S EXPERIENCE

Mapping the customer's experience starts by breaking it down into three main phases:

- **The Struggle phase:** your customer realizes they have a problem and begins seeking and exploring possible solutions
- **The Evaluation phase:** your customer commits to try your product and decides it's the solution they were looking for
- **The Growth phase:** your customer successfully embeds your product into their daily life and even may use it in *new* ways beyond the scope of the original problem.

STRUGGLE	EVALUATION	GROWTH

Within each phase, there are three questions you'll answer using your customer data:

- What is the customer thinking as they struggle, evaluate, and grow?
- What is the customer **doing** as they struggle, evaluate, and grow?

- What is the customer *feeling* as they struggle, evaluate, and grow?

	STRUGGLE	EVALUATION	GROWTH
Thinking			
Doing			
Feeling			

Knowing what someone is thinking gives us a window into what they're likely **doing** and why they're doing it. If we know what someone is thinking, we can also capture how they're likely *feeling*. Identifying these three aspects of a customer's emotional journey helps us understand (1) the milestones they reach in each phase and (2) when each milestone begins and ends.

	STRUGGLE		EVALUATION		GROWTH	
	Milestone	Milestone	Milestone	Milestone	Milestone	Milestone
Thinking						
Doing						
Feeling						

MAP YOUR CUSTOMER INSIGHTS

With an understanding of how you'll deconstruct your customers' experience into its parts, let's talk about how you'll use your research to map *your* customers' experience.

You'll find a more detailed guide in the workbook, but in brief, here are the steps:

1. On a whiteboard, you'll add a heading for each phase: Struggle, Evaluation, and Growth.
2. Referencing the customer data you collected for **your top priority customer Job**, you'll create sticky notes (since they're easy to move around) to add to your whiteboard.
3. Under each phase heading of Struggle, Evaluation, and Growth, you'll place the stickies that capture what the customer was thinking, doing, and feeling in that phase.
4. Then you'll identify the milestones within each phase.

We'll use the research done for a tool called SparkToro as a reference to explain these steps in more detail. SparkToro is an audience research tool for marketers co-founded by friend (and client), Rand Fishkin, founder and former CEO of Moz.

Here's SparkToro's ideal customer's Job:

> **When I'm** exploring or optimizing a marketing channel, **give me** easy access to useful, compelling insights **so I can** gain clarity, take action, and impress my stakeholders.

Let's dig in.

Mapping Struggle Phase Insights

At the beginning of the Struggle phase, your customer is still doing things the old way. They're using a different solution, or maybe doing nothing. Then, something happens that causes them to realize that they have a problem, and that what they're doing now isn't working anymore. They look around for solutions, somehow find your product, and make the leap to take things to the next level.

This "struggle speak" will sound pretty familiar by now. You've already identified the struggles that push your customers to seek a solution like yours. You've created a customer job statement summarizing each and picked one to prioritize. This next step is about *pulling apart* that top-priority struggle into the real actions your customers take as they look for solutions.

Let's reference the struggle that SparkToro's customers feel: *"When I'm exploring or optimizing a marketing channel..."* How do they realize they have a problem? Whose advice do they seek? What keywords do they use?

Questions you ask in your research (covered in Chapters 3 and 4) will give you insight into what your customers with this Job were thinking, what they were doing, and how they were feeling during their Struggle phase. Those questions include:

- When did you first start using [product name]?
- Take me back to life before [product name]. Prior to [product name], what were you using instead? If you were using a combination of any tools or products, what were those?
- Tell me about the moment you realized [old way] wasn't cutting it. What caused that moment? What compelled you to look for something different?
- Where did you go to look for new solutions? Did you try anything else before [product name]?
- How did you find out about [product name]?
- Why did you decide to choose [product name] over other options? Can you recall anything that stood out to you?

Let's look at survey responses from SparkToro's customers that give us insight into their Struggle phase.

Survey question: When did you realize you needed something like SparkToro? What was going on in your world that caused you to start looking for something new?

Answers from customers, revealing what they were thinking:

- *"My clients started asking questions I couldn't answer."*
- *"I mainly scraped Twitter and other social media channels."*
- *"We were just looking for a more efficient way to tap into audience insights [compared with our manual process]."*
- *"My client was having a hard time finding success with ad targeting strategies."*
- *"A majority of our persona building, audience research, and outreach planning involved far too much subjectivity and guesswork."*

From those answers, we can tell what customers were likely **doing:**

- Pitching to and meeting with clients
- Manually scraping and mining social media
- Searching for audience research tools
- Running ads for clients
- Extracting terms, hashtags, trending news

And what they were likely *feeling:*

- Frustrated
- Stressed

The trick is to **read between the lines** of customers' answers. For example, from the statement "my client started asking questions I couldn't answer," we know this customer is managing clients, that they're trying to make clients happy, and that they might feel stressed or frustrated.

Repeat this "unpacking" process for all of the questions asked that give insight into what customers with this Job were thinking, doing, and feeling during their Struggle phase.

Mapping Evaluation Phase Insights

Once your customer has made that first commitment to try out your product—starting a trial, requesting a demo, etc.—they've moved into the Evaluation phase. They might land inside your product for the first time. They might dig through your help docs. They may meet with a sales rep for a demo. Eventually, they get to an "aha" moment: they take some set of actions using your product that helps them realize, "Hey, this thing might actually solve my problem." They haven't bought it yet, but are most definitely interested.

With initial confidence established, they go a step further: they might invite team members into the product or poke around to make sure you do indeed have all their mission-critical features. Once they're fully bought in that your product *can* solve their problem, they're ready to commit—whether by inputting their credit card details or pitching and getting approval from higher-ups.

Questions from your research that give you insight into the Evaluation phase include:

- Why did you decide to choose [product name] over other options? Can you recall anything that stood out to you?
- When you signed up for [product name], what happened that made you feel certain it was the right solution for you?
- Now that you have [product name], what's the number one thing you're able to do that you weren't before?

Note: There may be some overlapping. That is, some questions may provide data that's helpful in multiple phases (like both Struggle and Evaluation, for example). That's totally okay and even expected. As you go, you'll get better at spotting when that happens.

Here are some Evaluation phase insights from SparkToro's customers:

Survey question: Why did you decide to choose SparkToro over other options? Can you recall anything that stood out to you?

Answers from customers, revealing what they were thinking:

- *"The interface is dead simple, which helped a ton."*
- *"I found great sites to guest post on, and had data that showed why we should prioritize them."*
- *"The founders came across as genuinely trying to help folks."*

Here's another example:

Survey question: When you signed up for SparkToro, what

happened that made you feel certain it was the right solution for you?

Answers from customers, revealing what they were <u>thinking</u>:

- *"I saw how quickly I could put together outreach lists and build primary and secondary audiences to inform marketing strategy."*
- *"Better customer insight—fast—for example, before talking to a new client."*
- *"I realized that it saves me and my team a lot of time."*

From these answers, we can tell what customers were likely **doing**:

- Going through product tour
- Running first search
- Evaluating first search results
- Trying different search types
- Creating lists
- Re-running previous search queries and browsing results
- Exporting profile email contacts
- Comparing audiences
- Analyzing specific websites and social accounts

And *feeling*:

- Hopeful
- Relieved
- Excited

Make sure to repeat this process for all the questions you

asked in your research that will give you insight into your customer's Evaluation phase. After you've figured out what your customers are thinking, doing, and feeling here, it's time to move on to the Growth phase.

Mapping Growth Phase Insights

You've helped your new customer solve their Job! But their relationship with your product has only just begun. At the start of the Growth phase, your customer is in the process of building habits around using your product. Only once your product has been *embedded* into their daily life or recurring workflows has their problem really been solved for good.

But this isn't where the story ends. Your customer will *evolve*. New struggles will arise for them; they'll have new challenges to tackle. If your product can continually solve *new* problems for your customer, then congratulations: you have a customer for life.

Questions you ask in your research that give you insight into their Growth phase:

- How are you using [product name] day-to-day?
- Now that you have [product name], what's the number one thing you're able to do that you weren't able to do before?
- What do you wish [product name] did that it doesn't do today?

Here are a few Growth phase insights from SparkToro's customers:

Survey question: Now that you have SparkToro, what's the number one thing you're able to do that you weren't able to do before?

Answers from customers, revealing what they were thinking:

- *"I can show my clients a faster, better way to get the market research they need done."*
- *"I'm 3x faster than my previous method and making 3x what I was before."*
- *"It is so easy to onboard more people to SparkToro when I am hiring—I want to help my team be as efficient and fast as possible."*

From those answers, we can tell what customers were likely **doing**:

- Creating new lists for each client's audience(s)
- Browsing results and adding to lists
- Adding team members
- Adding new clients

And *feeling*:

- Confident
- Determined

Again, repeat this process for all of the questions you asked that give you a view into what customers are thinking, doing, and feeling in their Growth phase.

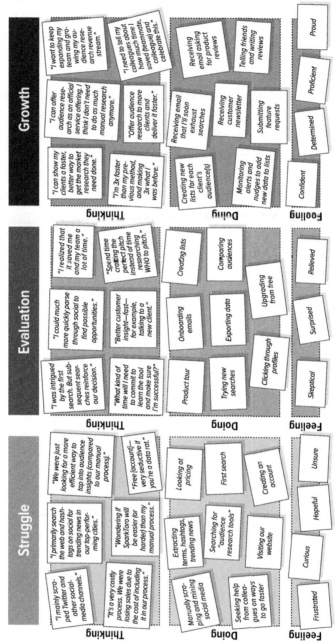

Figure 6.1. SparkToro's CX map of the Struggle, Evaluation, and Growth phases

As you're reading between the lines, you might see ways that your product or solution could evolve beyond just solving their original Job. "Sharing results externally with clients" is one example. Here, SparkToro could build new reporting features that make sharing results easier. That's how you know this process is working: you're using customer responses to figure out what customers actually need, and when.

Figure 6.1 shows what it might look like when you use stickies to create your CX map. For more in-depth instructions on how to populate your CX map with customer data, as usual, check out the workbook.

With the thinking, doing, and feeling stickies added to each phase on your board, you can move on to identifying the *milestones* within each phase.

IDENTIFY CUSTOMER MILESTONES

Milestones are the "leaps of faith" your customer takes throughout their relationship with you. They're the frame-by-frame storyboard of your ideal customer's journey; they progress through each milestone one at a time as they move forward in the process of becoming your best customer and beyond.

Identifying Struggle Phase Milestones

A helpful way to identify where different milestones begin and end in a phase is to look for similar *feelings* within a phase. As the customer shifts from one milestone to another, their feelings typically shift as well.

In the Struggle phase, look for those feeling-related patterns and group them together. The goal is to rearrange your stickies to show how the customer's mental and emotional state changes—from the beginning of the Struggle phase to the transition into the Evaluation phase. The table at the end of this section will help you visualize what Struggle phase milestones could look like. There's no one right number of milestones per phase—two or three is common, but it will ultimately depend on your product and how your team operates.

When pulling apart *feelings*—and then their corresponding thinking and **doing** stickies—the Struggle phase will often break down into at least two milestones:

1. A **problem** milestone where the customer feels *frustrated* ("This isn't working") or *stressed* ("I shouldn't be spending so much time doing this").
2. An **interest** milestone where they see a potential solution and either feel *hopeful* ("Here's something that could fix my problem!") or *skeptical* ("But is this really going to work for me?").

When customers shift from only feeling the problem to realizing there are potential solutions, their actions change. They begin to read product reviews, ask advice from coworkers and friends, visit competitor websites, search online, and look at pricing.

The following table shows how the responses from Spark-Toro customers are categorized into milestones in line with what they were thinking, doing, and feeling in the Struggle phase. Remember to read the columns from top to bottom (versus reading the rows left to right).

STRUGGLE

	PROBLEM MILESTONE	INTEREST MILESTONE
Thinking	*"My clients started asking questions I couldn't answer."* *"I mainly scraped Twitter and other social media channels."* *"My client was having a hard time finding success with ad targeting strategies."* *"It's a very costly process. We were losing sales due to the cost of including it in our process."*	*"We were just looking for a more efficient way to tap into audience insights [compared with our manual process]."* *"Could a tool like SparkToro improve my efficiency, time, and reduce costs?"* *"Wondering if SparkToro will be easier (or harder) than my manual process."*
Doing	• Manually scraping and mining social media • Extracting terms, hashtags, trending news • Running ads for clients • Pitching to and meeting with clients • Searching for "audience research tools"	• Watching homepage video • Visiting "how it works" page • Visiting plans page and learning about free account • Conducting first search • Creating account
Feeling	• Frustrated • Stressed	• Hopeful • Curious

Identifying Evaluation Phase Milestones

Finding milestones for the Evaluation phase follows the same process as the Struggle phase: group similar feelings to identify milestones.

The number of milestones in the Evaluation phase tends to vary more than in the Struggle phase because it will depend on the complexity of the needs of your customer and your product.

For example, if you target enterprise customers, there are a number of factors that influence your customer's evaluation process:

- A bigger and more complex company structure with multiple layers of stakeholders involved
- Meeting stringent security or technical needs
- Many team members needing onboarding

If you target small business customers, on the other hand, it's less likely that they have multiple layers of stakeholders involved or as many team members needing onboarding. They may care more about:

- being able to self-evaluate the solution;
- getting to value quickly; and
- not needing to talk to sales or support.

When pulling apart *feelings*—and then their corresponding thinking and **doing** stickies—depending on your customer's needs, the Evaluation phase will often break down into milestones like:

1. **Activation, often referred to as the "aha" moment**, or **First Value:** where customers experience value for the first time
2. **Engagement, or Value Realization:** where customers have solved the problem they came to your product to solve.

Here's how the responses from SparkToro customers are categorized into milestones in line with what they were thinking, doing, and feeling in the Evaluation phase:

EVALUATION

	FIRST VALUE MILESTONE	VALUE REALIZATION MILESTONE
Thinking	*"The interface is dead simple, which helped a ton."* *"I found great sites to guest post on, and had data that showed why we should prioritize them."* *"What kind of time will I need to commit to learn the tool and make sure I'm successful?"* *"Once we started going over our free credits it made sense to purchase a license."*	*"I saw how quickly I could put together outreach long-lists and build primary and secondary audiences to inform marketing strategy"* *"Better customer insight—fast—for example, before talking to a new client"* *"I realized that it saves me and my team a lot of time"*
Doing	• Going through the product tour • Running first search • Evaluating first search results • Trying different search types • Creating first list • Upgrading to a paid plan	• Re-running previous search queries and browsing results • Exporting profile email contacts, list data, and downloading CSVs • Comparing audiences • Analyzing specific websites and social accounts • Importing custom audiences
Feeling	• Skeptical • Hopeful	• Relieved • Excited

Identifying Growth Phase Milestones

Finding your customer's milestones for the Growth phase follows the same process as finding milestones for the previous phases. But for recurring revenue businesses, the Growth phase is especially important. **Everything rests on our ability to deliver continued value to customers.**

Like before, group similar feelings to find your customer milestones. Again, the number of milestones here depends on your customer. What are they able to do now that they couldn't do before? What does this "better life" look like for them? Also, what opportunities do they have to *expand* their usage or need for your product? Can you see ways to drive up value for your customer, or generate word-of-mouth referrals that will help attract more *new* customers?

When pulling apart *feelings*—and then their corresponding thinking and **doing** stickies—depending on your customer's needs, the Growth phase will often be broken down into milestones like:

1. **Engagement**, or **Continued Value:** where it's clear that customers have established a habit and your product is embedded into their life.
2. **Expansion**, or **Value Growth:** where customers evolve in their needs, expand their usage, become a "pro," and/ or begin telling others about your solution.

Here's how the responses from SparkToro customers are categorized into milestones in line with what they were thinking, doing, and feeling in the Growth phase:

	CONTINUED VALUE MILESTONE	VALUE GROWTH MILESTONE
Thinking	*"I can show my clients a faster, better way to get the market research they need done."* *"I'm 3x faster than my previous method and making 3x what I was before."* *"It is so easy to onboard more people to SparkToro when I am hiring—I want to help my team be as efficient and fast as possible."*	*"I like to only do what matters. The noise of unnecessary research steps and data are eliminated. I've narrowed my process down to just the three top activities."* *"I want to keep expanding my team and growing my audience research revenue stream."* *"I need to tell my colleagues about how much time I saved and celebrate this."*
Doing	• Conducting more searches • Browsing results and adding to lists • Creating new lists for client's audience(s) • Exporting profile email contacts, list data, and downloading CSVs • Comparing audiences • Analyzing specific websites and social accounts • Importing custom audiences • Adding team members • Adding new clients	• Receiving alert that monthly searches will be exhausted (when applicable) • Exhausting allotted searches and upgrading to next tier • Receiving emails with referral incentive • Receiving emails asking for product reviews/case studies and leaving reviews • Submitting feature requests
Feeling	• Confident • Determined	• Proud • Proficient • Impactful

Figure 6.2. A complete CX map

	Struggle		Evaluation		Growth	
	Problem	**Interest**	**First Value**	**Value Realization**	**Continued Value**	**Value Growth**
Thinking	*"My clients are asking questions I can't answer."* *"Scraping Twitter is so time-consuming."* *"There has to be a better way."*	*"Will SparkToro be easier than my manual process?"* *"How much does it cost?"* *"The first free search is cool."*	*"What king of time will I need to commit to learn SparkToro?"* *"Wow, I wouldn't have found these insights on my own."*	*"This will save me and my team so much time."* *"Now I can spend time crafting the perfect pitch, instead of figuring out WHO to pitch."*	*"I'm 3x faster than my previous method, and making 3x what I was before."* *"I can show my clients a better way to get the research they need done."*	*"I can offer audience research as an official service offering."* *"I want to expand my team and grow my audience research revenue."*
Doing	Manually scraping social media · Seeking help from colleagues on ways to go faster · Searching for "audience research tools"	Visiting our website · Looking at pricing · First search · Creating an account	Product tour · Onboarding emails · Trying new searches · Clicking through profiles	Creating lists · Comparing audiences · Exporting data · Upgrading from free	Creating new lists for each client's audience(s) · Monitoring alerts and nudges to add new data to lists · Receiving email that I'll soon exhaust searches	Receiving customer newsletter · Submitting feature requests · Receiving email asking for product reviews · Telling friends and writing reviews
Feeling						

WHERE THE MAGIC HAPPENS

Unlike transaction-centered buyer journey maps, customer experience mapping focuses on *your* ideal customer's *real experience* with your unique product and business model.

Your CX map isn't based on assumptions but on value customers *actually* report. It enables not just your CLG Team, but *your entire company* to see and understand what your customer experiences as they evolve in their relationship with your solution.

With your customers' unique milestones in hand, you and your team will finally be able to identify exactly where you're meeting customer's needs well, and where you're dropping the ball.

This is where the magic happens.

Teresa Torres, Product Discovery Coach, says: "Because maps help us externalize our ideas and relieve our working memory, we often uncover unintended consequences of our ideas—which can lead to better ideas."

In other words, a common "aha" moment for CLG Teams in the mapping process is "Oh, shit, we haven't been doing X," which quickly turns into, "Oh, shit, look at all the amazing opportunities we have to do X, Y, Z, and more."

But before you can start implementing all the opportunities bouncing around in your brain, you have to decide how you'll **measure the success** of those opportunities. What outcomes and goals will you be shooting for? What are your targets? How will you track and quantify them?

So let's talk about defining key performance indicators, or KPIs, in the next chapter.

Chapter 7

IDENTIFYING CUSTOMER-LED KPIS

In her early days of working in SaaS, Claire knew some folks at another fast-growing startup who were dealing with a sticky situation.

The company's marketing team and outbound sales team were both responsible for the same metric: qualified leads. But instead of working collaboratively to hit their targets, the opposite was happening.

It had recently been discovered that the outbound Sales Manager, struggling to get his reps to hit their monthly quotas, had been reporting all of the marketing-generated qualified leads as outbound sales-generated. Not only did this naturally lead to finger pointing and tension between the two departments, but it had also been falsely inflating the company's revenue projections—dangerous territory, to say the least.

It's easy to assume the outbound Sales Manager is the problem here. But **in reality, the root of the problem is deeper and, sadly, quite common: unclear, poorly set KPIs.**

In the words of Eliyahu Goldratt, "Tell me how you will measure me, and then I will tell you how I will behave." Put a different way: when we're rewarded (or punished) for performance against a metric, we do what's needed to minimize our risk of punishment. And that means doing whatever is in our control.

In the marketing-vs.-outbound-sales situation, tying two departments' performance to the same goal led to confusion and ultimately bad behavior. And poorly set KPIs don't only create *internal* dysfunction; they can also wreak havoc on your *customer's* experience.

A common example is measuring a customer support team's performance by volume or speed of tickets closed. Optimizing for volume or speed is well intended; we all want speedy replies when we need help. But this opens the door for a negative customer experience. Support reps are incentivized to give quick, boilerplate responses—to potentially complex customer issues—so they can close the ticket and move on to the next one.

Unfortunately, "ticket closed" doesn't necessarily mean "problem solved." It doesn't mean the customer is happy with your product. It could even lead to the customer *firing* your product.

Which is why tying your team's performance *to your customer's success* is so valuable.

MEASURE CUSTOMER VALUE

A super-common metric for measuring customer engagement is daily, weekly, or monthly active users. The logic is that if a customer is logging into your product, then they're engaged. Simple to understand, easy to track.

Unfortunately for many products, this metric has nothing to do with the customer getting value, or moving from one milestone to the next, in their journey with your product.

Take FeedOtter, a newsletter automation tool for marketing managers. The beauty of FeedOtter is *not* having to log in: it runs in the background, eliminating the work of building, editing, and sending out newsletters manually.

If FeedOtter measured customer engagement by daily logins, the team would be incentivized to continually nudge customers back into the product. But as a customer, imagine how annoying it would be to get "Don't forget to log in!" notifications when the reason you signed up in the first place was to give yourself one *less* task to do.

FeedOtter's customer research showed that what their best customers wanted—what was *valuable to them*—was speed and simplicity. Customers wanted a consistent way to get their content out to their audience so that they could focus on the content creation itself.

Once you know what your customer values, you can start measuring your success based on customers taking actions that show you they *received* that value. For a FeedOtter customer, logging in isn't it. A more value-aligned metric would be when a customer's newsletters are consistently automated, error-free.

MEASURE WHAT YOU CAN ACT ON

Let's talk about lagging indicators of success vs. leading indicators of success.

Lagging indicators represent *results*. They help you understand the economics of your business. They're often dollar amounts: annual or monthly recurring revenue, your cost to acquire a customer, average revenue per user, customer lifetime value, etc.

Lagging indicators are critical to keep an eye on, of course. They're just not actionable. They tell you what's happened, but they don't tell you *why*, or *what* your team should do next.

Leading indicators are metrics you *can* act on. They represent *actions* your customers take that, when tracked, help you understand their success with your solution—or lack thereof, where they're dropping out.

Here are some common leading and lagging indicators for comparison:

LEADING INDICATORS (ACTION)	LAGGING INDICATORS (RESULT)
• New unique visits • Signups • Product activation • Product engagement • Product expansion • Referrals, reviews • Net promoter score (NPS) • Customer satisfaction rating (CSAT)	• Annual or monthly recurring revenue (ARR/MRR) • Cost to acquire a customer (CAC) • Average revenue per user (ARPU) • Customer lifetime value (CLV/LTV)

When you improve the right leading indicator metrics, your lagging indicator metrics improve as a result. This is why it's so important to use leading indicators when assigning metrics to your CX milestones.

DEFINE A KPI FOR EACH MILESTONE

If each milestone in your CX map represents a step your customer takes along their journey with you, then you'll need a way to measure how customers are moving from one to the next. So each milestone needs a KPI that indicates a customer has successfully taken that step.

To make this process more tangible, we'll reference Spark-Toro's CX map.

STRUGGLE PHASE KPIS

To get started, look at the first milestone in your CX map, which we refer to as the **Problem** milestone. What actions do customers take within this milestone that indicate your potential customers are making progress and that the team is doing a good job?

For SparkToro (as with most companies), that action is **the customer visiting their website for the first time.** It's trackable. It represents someone initially finding out about SparkToro. And finally, it shows that the team's efforts are paying off: people are clicking on ads, or seeing SparkToro in their search results, or getting to the site through whatever channels the team may use to build awareness.

The KPI that represents this customer action is "new unique website visits." Note the intentional focus on *new unique* visits, which represents building awareness with *new* people. The more commonly measured "traffic" would represent everyone: existing customers who are just there to log in, frequent readers of their blog, etc.

STRUGGLE		EVALUATION	GROWTH
Problem	Interest		
New unique website visitor			

Moving to the next milestone in your CX map, which we refer to as **Interest**, ask yourself what your customer is **doing** that:

- you can track;
- implies that they've transitioned from initial curiosity to actually wanting to explore your product (a leap of faith);
- tips them into the Evaluation phase once the action is complete; and
- indicates that you've done a good job helping them reach value.

One common action that shows interest is your customer completing your website's primary call to action, whether that's a free trial signup, app download, or a demo request. For SparkToro, the action is their customer using the product's search bar for the first time.

STRUGGLE		EVALUATION	GROWTH
Problem	Interest		
New unique website visitor	**First search**		

Evaluation Phase KPIs

Here's where defining KPIs gets a little more interesting. A potential customer is inside your product for the first time; now what?

Back to your CX map. In your first Evaluation phase milestone, look for what customers said about:

- Why they chose your product over others—what stood out to them
- What happened that made them feel certain your product was the right solution
- What can they do now that they weren't able to before

You're going to match what your customers said was valuable to the features and attributes of your product that *create* **that value.**

For SparkToro customers, what stood out was:

- how easy it was to run a search;
- how useful and compelling search results were;
- the ability to organize search results for reference later; and
- the ability to share insights with their team and clients.

SparkToro's features and product attributes that *created* that value for customers were:

- in-depth search results;
- filters and sorting features;
- list functionality; and
- export functionality.

The following table maps customer value to SparkToro's features and product attributes in a more visual way:

CUSTOMER VALUE	FEATURES AND PRODUCT ATTRIBUTES THAT HELP CREATE THAT VALUE
How easy it is to run a search	In-depth search results
How useful and compelling search results are	Filters and sorting features
The ability to organize search results for reference later	List functionality
The ability to share insights with their team and clients	Export functionality

Before we can decide how we want to *introduce* our solution to potential customers, we need to be clear on **how our product helps them solve their problem.** We call this the **Value Realization** milestone: it's **when everything** *clicks into place* **for them, and it's your best indicator that they've felt value and will likely become a paying customer.**

For SparkToro, we can see that customers felt value when they used the filters, lists, and export features. This means finding and using those features are key in customers' adoption of the product and decision to pay.

So SparkToro defined their Value Realization KPI as "10+ searches *and* 2+ lists created *and* 1+ exports generated."

STRUGGLE		EVALUATION		GROWTH
Problem	Interest	First Value	Value Realization	
New unique website visitor	First search		10+ searches *and* 2+ lists *and* 1+ exports	

Since Value Realization is when your customer has solved their Job, it's typically one of the later milestones in the Evaluation phase, if not the last. It's rare, if ever, that a customer will go from landing in your product for the first time straight to "Hell yes, this is right for me."

Before customers can get to full Value Realization, **they need a sign that they're on the right track.** We call this the **First Value** milestone. Your First Value KPI should measure **customers getting a tempting glimpse of the value that's to come. That typically means learning about the features that will help them solve their problem.**

SparkToro's First Value KPI became "5+ searches *and* 1+ lists created" because that set of actions gave new customers a chance to explore search results and organize those results into a list.

STRUGGLE		EVALUATION		GROWTH
Problem	Interest	First Value	Value Realization	
New unique website visitor	First search	5+ searches *and* 1+ lists	10+ searches and 2+ lists *and* 1+ exports	

Growth Phase KPIs

Your customer makes it all the way through Struggle and Evaluation, and into the Growth phase. What next?

When SparkToro's customers were asked what they could do now that they had a solution to their problem, they said:

- They had clarity on what influences their clients' audiences (what they listen to, watch, and read).
- They were better able to target the right audiences.
- They could quickly call up and share results.
- They could exceed expectations and even have a competitive advantage over others in their space.

Same as before, the following table maps SparkToro's features and product attributes to the value they create for customers:

CUSTOMER VALUE	FEATURES AND PRODUCT ATTRIBUTES THAT HELP CREATE THAT VALUE
Clarity on what influences their clients' audiences (what they listen to, watch, and read)	In-depth search results
Better able to target the right audiences	Filters and sorting features
Could quickly call up and share results	Lists and data exporting
Could exceed expectations and even have a competitive advantage over others in their space	Depth and speed of results

For most companies, the conversion point to paying customer happens when customers transition from Evaluation to Growth. Your customer felt enough value to start paying for your product. **But to keep them around, you need to *continually* deliver value.** This is mission critical for recurring revenue-based businesses like SaaS—if you're not retaining customers, you're not in business.

We call this first Growth phase milestone **Continued Value.** The KPI for Continued Value should represent your customer getting value in an *ongoing* way. You might want to combine customer actions with a time range or frequency: how often your healthy customers tend to take those actions.

For SparkToro, the Continued Value KPI became:

- The Value Realization KPI (10+ searches *and* 2+ lists *and* 1+ exports *or* key feature usage)...
- On a **monthly** basis

This way, SparkToro **knows** they're successfully delivering continued value to their customers, month over month.

STRUGGLE		EVALUATION		GROWTH	
Problem	Interest	First Value	Value Realization	Continued Value	Value Growth
New unique website visitor	First search	5+ searches and 1+ lists	10+ searches and 2+ lists and 1+ exports	Monthly 10+ searches and 2+ lists and 1+ exports	

Once your customer is getting continued value, things *really* get interesting. They've solved the problem that originally brought them to your product; now, what *new* challenges can you solve for them? How else can you deliver value?

There are many possibilities for the **Value Growth** milestone. This may be the point at which your customer is ready to:

- use features that require an upgrade to the next pricing tier;
- switch from monthly to annual billing;
- invite more team members to their account;
- join your referral or affiliate program;
- leave a five-star review or write a glowing testimonial;
- become a power user of your product; and
- invite and teach others about it.

Whether by expanding their own usage or their team's usage, or by telling everyone they know about your product and bringing additional customers through the front door, recurring revenue businesses defy normal growth at this milestone. Value Growth is when the potential for expansion or net revenue retention (NRR) finally becomes clearer.

For SparkToro, the Value Growth KPI became:

- The Continued Value KPI (Monthly 10+ searches *and* 2+ lists *and* 1+ exports *or* key feature usage)...
- *And* **upgrade** *or* **review** *or* **referral.**

STRUGGLE		EVALUATION		GROWTH	
Problem	Interest	First Value	Value Realization	Continued Value	Value Growth
New unique website visitor	First search	5+ searches *and* 1+ lists	10+ searches *and* 2+ lists *and* 1+ exports	Monthly 10+ searches *and* 2+ lists *and* 1+ exports	**Monthly 10+ searches *and* 2+ lists *and* 1+ exports *and* upgrade *or* review *or* referral**

THERE'S NO GOING BACK

Your tool kit is complete.

You've done the research. You've identified your best customers' Job. You understand the phases of the customer's journey, the milestones they encounter with your product, and the customer-led KPIs needed to measure progress.

You're on the precipice of predictable, meaningful growth.

Don't fuck it up.

Don't fall into the trap of doing what you've always done. Don't just talk about your shiny new customer-led KPIs; champion them. **Use them.**

Build dashboards for your customer KPIs (Figure 7.1). This creates visibility for all into the health of your customers:

how you're successfully meeting **customers' needs**—or not. And **start benchmarking your performance.** Tracking how well you're currently bridging the success gaps between milestones will help you prioritize your opportunities for growth (covered in the next chapter).

New Uniques	First Searches	Activated
15k	**2,382**	**325**
↑ 33%	↑ 12%	↑ 40%
vs last week	vs last week	vs last week
Newly Engaged	Engaged	Expansion
204	**4,898**	**$8,325**
↓ 05%	↑ 08%	↑ 37%
vs last week	vs last week	vs last week

Figure 7.1. KPI dashboard example

Once these new KPIs are established, you can **release your team into the world confident that they're willing, able, and prepared to move in a direction that drives customer value**—which will inherently drive revenue.

KPIs in hand, now you can look at what you're currently doing to serve customers and identify the biggest opportunities to improve. It's time to operationalize.

YOUR TURN

Take stock of the metrics you've been using to date. Which are leading indicators of success, and which are lagging indicators of success? It's time to make sure your team's efforts are measured in a way they can act on. In a way that's tied to customer value. In a way that drives predictable growth.

1. In your CX map, review what customers say is important to them (thinking) and the measurable action they are taking (**doing**).
2. For each milestone, identify the customer-led KPIs that measure your ability to drive customer's success.
3. Build a dashboard for visibility and start benchmarking your performance.

Find helpful guides and templates at forgetthefunnel.com/workbook.

Part IV

OPERATIONALIZING YOUR CUSTOMER INSIGHTS

Chapter 8

BRIDGING CUSTOMERS' SUCCESS GAPS

With SparkToro's KPIs established, it was clear: their customers were getting to the Problem and Interest milestones just fine, but many were struggling to reach First Value.

STRUGGLE		EVALUATION		GROWTH	
Problem	Interest	First Value	Value Realization	Continued Value	Value Growth
New unique website visitor	First search	5+ searches *and* 1+ lists	10+ searches *and* 2+ lists *and* 1+ exports	Monthly 10+ searches *and* 2+ lists *and* 1+ exports	Monthly 10+ searches *and* 2+ lists *and* 1+ exports *and* upgrade *or* review *or* referral
Lots of people were getting here	and here...	but way fewer were getting here			

We'd learned from research what SparkToro's best customers valued: ease of use and actionable insights. We knew their desired outcome: gain the clarity needed to take action and impress their boss or their client. We knew the exact features that helped them achieve that desired outcome.

But when potential customers got into the product for the first time, many of them weren't finding and using those features. As a result, they weren't reaching those critical value moments.

To make it easier for potential customers to reach First Value, SparkToro *(shout-out to VP Marketing Amanda Natividad!)* made two significant changes to their customer experience:

1. They built an in-app checklist to help new users find those key features.
2. They wrote an onboarding email series, based on insights and messaging pulled from customer responses, to help new users get the most out of those key features.

Two months after launching these updates, SparkToro's free-to-paid conversions had *doubled*—a 100% increase.

Launching an in-app checklist and an email series are examples of bridging a **success gap—a disconnect between what your ideal customers need and want, and what your customer experience provides.**

Before you run wild with whatever idea sounds the most fun or trendy or interesting, you need to **identify the biggest success gaps your ideal customers face across your customer experience.**

STEP 1: IDENTIFY SUCCESS GAPS

The most straightforward way to begin identifying success gaps is to **put yourself in the shoes of an ideal customer who needs your product.** Doing this as a group with your CLG Team will be extra valuable, since more eyes means more chances to spot gaps between what your ideal customers need and want, and what your current customer experience provides.

Refresh your memory on your top-priority customer Job, then go through each milestone of your CX map as they would.

Literally. Go *do* the things your ideal customer does in the Problem milestone, as they're experiencing the pain. Review the places they go when they begin their search for a new solution. Look at the marketing campaigns you're running to reach that potential customer.

When you started this book, you wanted clarity on where to focus. Walking through your customer's experience, *in your ideal customer's shoes*, gives you that clarity. **You'll see all the mismatches between what "good" would look like for your customer and the experience you provide today.**

Once you've done all the things your customer does in the Problem milestone, move to the Interest milestone. Look at your homepage or other key landing pages they may be visiting. You now know your ideal customer's desired outcome; **does your value proposition make it clear that your product can help them achieve it?** You know the features they care most and least about; **are you introducing the most import-ant features first**, or—like Autobooks used to do—are you throwing all of them out there at once? You know the pain points and anxieties they're dealing with; **is it obvious how your product addresses the typical objections?**

Continue walking through the entire experience until you've reached the final KPI. In addition to all the fantastic opportunities your team dreams up while building your CX map, you'll *also* now have a long list of friction points you caught during this walkthrough.

You're finally in a good place to decide which success gap needs urgent attention.

STEP 2: CHOOSE ONE SUCCESS GAP

To decide where to focus, answer this question: **which success gap is causing the most harm to your customer's experience?** In other words, which gap, if bridged first, would increase the impact of your other opportunities?

Choose the success gap where **even a modest increase in conversion rates would generate an outsized impact on revenue.** You can often spot these by noting a high volume of customers reaching one milestone but few making it through to the next. If you're struggling to make a call, ask yourself which KPI, if your team improved on it, would:

- have the biggest potential financial payoff;
- leverage the existing team, resources, and budget best;
- be actionable in the short term (if not immediately) and;
- excite the team because they already have a clear path to fix the experience.

Or, as Gary Keller asks in his book *The ONE Thing*: "What's the one thing you can do, such that by doing it, everything else will be easier or unnecessary?"[2]

STEP 3: GET CLEAR ON HOW YOU'LL BRIDGE THE GAP

During CX mapping (covered in Chapter 6), it's likely that you'll come up with a ton of ideas to make your customer's experience better. Now is the time to explore those ideas and give them life.

All ideas are now on the table, as long as they *directly* *help* bridge the top-priority success gap chosen in Step 2—whether you came up with them during CX map creation, or when you audited the end-to-end customer experience. For now, put opportunities that bridge other success gaps on the shelf; with clarity on your top priority comes *focus*.

There may be dozens of ideas you *could* pursue, but some will have greater impact than others. Try to whittle your options down to just a handful of projects that you can confidently knock out within the next few weeks or months.

To get juices flowing, here are some common projects teams use to bridge success gaps:

---

2   Gary Keller and Jay Papasan, *The One Thing: The Surprising Simple Truth Behind Extraordinary Results* (Austin, TX: Bard Press, 2013).

STRUGGLE		EVALUATION		GROWTH	
Problem	Interest	First Value	Value Realization	Continued Value	Value Growth
Ad/ marketing campaigns Thought leadership content Referral programs Partner programs	Website messaging Pricing updates CTA (call to action) updates (e.g., *Try it free* instead of *Schedule a demo*)	In-app onboarding updates Product tour Email onboarding Training webinars	Win-back nurture emails "Why wasn't [product] right for you?" emails	Additional feature-based or use case-based nurture sequences Continuous customer education content and events	Add-on or upgrade nurture emails Annual subscription nurture Product reviews or referrals (soliciting)

Once you've chosen the projects you'll pursue to bridge the biggest success gap, **you'll measure your impact using your newly defined KPIs.**

STEP 4: MAKE SHIT HAPPEN

At this point, you know:

- exactly where to focus in your customers' experience to move the needle on revenue;
- which projects will have the biggest impact on your customers' success (and therefore your business's) and;
- how you'll measure success as you execute.

As your team switches into execution mode, *don't lose sight of what you've built here.* Prioritize your new KPIs. Schedule recurring CX health-checks with your team. With these tools in hand, you have what you need to continually, consistently bridge success gaps and deliver greater value. **Where there is customer value to add, there is revenue to gain.**

If you need some inspiration, we have a few more success stories for you from teams who've operationalized customer-led growth:

Using the Customer-Led Growth Framework, **CareerCake's** then-Head of Marketing, Lucy Heskins, DIYed her way to a customer experience map, KPIs, and marketing campaigns. She revised the messaging and copy used across her lead nurture program. As a result, she reduced the average time required to convince leads to book sales calls from one month to three days. **That's a 90% increase in velocity.**

Based on a clearer understanding of their best customers' Job, the team at **Life Lapse** rewrote their homepage to better match customers' struggles, motivations, and desired outcomes. **Website visitors converting to new users increased by 93%** (from 9.42% originally to 18.19%). These users were reaching First Value and Value Realization more quickly, too: **overall sales jumped 18.9% in just 50 days.**

HiringBranch updated messaging to match their best customers' language, highlighted features their best customers found most valuable, and offered a free trial after learning that customers wanted to test out the product themselves before making a decision. Following *months* with no inbound leads at all, **within just 12 days of their new site going live, they got four qualified inbound leads from multimillion dollar prospects.**

Imagine what *you* could do if, every month or quarter, you bridged a new success gap and improved performance against another KPI. And we're just talking *one* CX map, *one* customer Job. Don't forget the others you have the opportunity to explore.

When you use your CX map and KPIs to focus and guide your strategies, you'll see your performance move up and to the right each time.

In the next chapter, we'll discuss ways to integrate customer-led growth across an organization so that it becomes a permanent part of how you and your team operate.

YOUR TURN

Before you can jump into executing all your great ideas, you need to slow down (just temporarily!) to speed up.

1. Refresh your memory on your top-priority customer Job. Act as your customer who's looking to "hire" your product for that Job and go through each milestone of your CX map.
2. Identify the biggest success gaps your ideal customers face in your current customer experience.
3. Decide which one success gap you can fix, such that by fixing it, every other success gap will benefit.

Find detailed guides on this process at forgetthefunnel.com/workbook.

Chapter 9

INTEGRATING AND ITERATING CUSTOMER-LED PRACTICES

You know why your best customers seek out a new solution, what problem they're really trying to solve, and why they choose *you.*

You know the stages of their journey and the KPIs that represent them getting value at each milestone.

You know where to focus to move the needle on revenue and which projects will make the greatest impact.

The biggest mistake you could make now is to put all that hard work on a shelf.

This chapter will help you make sure that doesn't happen.

SHARING YOUR CUSTOMER INSIGHTS AND CX MAP

If something looks like shit, people will treat it like shit. And unless your CLG Team includes a graphic designer, the initial version of your CX map will probably look a bit messy—meaning it'll be less likely to build trust and confidence company-wide.

If possible, get a professional designer's help. Or you can always grab the CX map template we've provided in the workbook.

Finalized CX map in hand, you can introduce this new tool to the team. Since your CX map visually represents the work of nearly everyone across the company, be sure to share it, whether in an all-hands meeting or some other company-wide communication, with *everyone*. Here's a rundown of what to cover to increase your chances of getting people bought-in and excited:

- **Reiterate the value** of this work to the business and connect it to revenue growth whenever possible (Chapter 1). Simply saying "Here's what we learned about our customers" doesn't prove why the work was important. What's in it for the rest of the company? Why should they care?

- **Call out all contributors** and give lots of thanks to everyone involved (Chapter 2). This helps build credibility and emphasizes that what's been done is valuable company-wide. It's *especially* important for the Primary Stakeholder to publicly show their support of this work.

- **Show off the data** that backs up the decisions made so far and the research methods you used to get you here (Chapters 3 and 4). Provide a highlight reel of the customer insights uncovered and your prioritized customer Job (Chapter 5).

- **Introduce the customer milestones** at a high level and show how the KPIs for each demonstrate customer value (Chapters 6 and 7).

- **Explain how the CX map will be used** in the short-, mid-, and long-term (Chapter 8, plus more later in this chapter).

- **Let everyone know that you're open to questions or challenges.** These are a good sign: they're an opportunity to help people connect the dots between your new insights and decisions, and how their own work can be positively impacted. The more company-wide discussion there is, the better.

Everyone on your team stands to benefit from your new-found customer insight and system for operationalizing customer success. As you've seen for yourself, this process doesn't just help solve marketing challenges: *everyone* stands to benefit, from Product and Customer Success to Sales and Finance. This map **democratizes the customer's experience** and serves as the source of truth for your entire organization.

BEING CUSTOMER-LED IN YOUR DAY-TO-DAY

We all know companies that claim to be customer-led, or that claim to always put the customer first. For many, those claims are bullshit. Being *truly* customer-led means focusing on the customer's experience *every single day*.

Leverage your top-priority customer Job and CX map as strategic decision-making tools across *all* departments as part of their day-to-day work. Here a few ideas to get you started:

- **Use the CX map to guide annual and quarterly planning.** Every department's annual or quarterly plan should state what customer Job and milestone their work supports, and which KPI will be impacted as a result. This limits random projects or tactics that eat up time and resources but don't contribute to the big picture.

- **Use the CX map to guide individual projects** within teams' larger plans. This can be as simple as adding one to two lines at the top of your company's project brief, stating what customer Job and milestone the project is designed to improve (and, as above, which KPI will be impacted).

- **Redefine teams' and individuals' targets.** Use the new KPIs you've defined to track performance on projects and daily tasks. As you see those KPIs improve, you'll see revenue grow as well.

- **Create accessible dashboards for your KPIs.** This goes for top-level KPIs as well as for important *nested* metrics within each individual milestone in your CX map. This helps teams celebrate each others' wins and builds a ton more accountability.

- **Contextualize research done by different teams**, at different points in time. Just like tying teams' projects to CX milestones, tie *research* back to the CX map. This gives people a better understanding of how learning from the research fits into the larger end-to-end customer experience. For example, the Marketing team may do audience research that informs your customer's Problem milestone. The Product team might do UX research that informs what's happening during First Value. The Customer Success team might run an NPS (net promoter score) survey to better understand what's going on during Value Growth.

- **Supercharge employee onboarding.** When you incorporate the CX map into your employee onboarding process, each new team member can quickly get up to speed on who your ideal customer is and the problem you solve for that customer. This builds empathy, fosters a customer-led mindset from the start, and—again—helps new hires see how *their* day-to-day work connects to the customer's experience.

The impact of making these changes is that every person, across every team, can put themselves in your customer's shoes during their daily work: as they come on board, as they plan, prepare project briefs, track targets, and more.

Once Gia and the team at Unbounce could rely on their CX map and company-wide understanding of customer milestones, meetings became simpler. The team no longer needed to level-set about project goals. KPIs were clear. Marketing, Customer Success, Sales, and Product all understood each others' roles in the customer experience.

This company-wide understanding of—and operationalizing around—your customer's experience helps everyone work toward a shared goal and move in the same direction together. And that team cohesion, at scale, is what leads to results like 864% revenue growth.

BEING CUSTOMER-LED MEANS GROWING AND EVOLVING

As your company scales, as your product matures, as customer markets shift or you break into new ones—however your company evolves—the Customer-Led Growth Framework is your blueprint for success.

There are two primary ways you may want to iterate or build on what you've done:

- Go back to your research, this time focusing on a customer Job you identified but tabled. Build a new CX map with KPIs that reflect the experience of customers who hire your product to solve that Job.

- Start the Customer-Led Growth Framework steps again, but this time for a customer segment you don't currently serve well, or for a new market you're ready to explore.

Whatever you do, don't let this work sit on a shelf. Your CX map can be your workhorse if you let it. It can carry context and insight like words in a meeting never could.

An article published by First Round Review describes how the company Guru (an internal knowledge-sharing platform for teams) puts their customer's success at the center of everything the team does. As First Round Review puts it, "Guru's approach to proving customer outcomes is meticulously quantified, rigorously unambiguous, and integrated into every facet of the company."[3]

That's the ultimate goal of the Customer-Led Growth Framework: **making your customer's experience quantifiable, unambiguous, and the bedrock of your organization—every department, every team, every decision.**

If you can achieve this, then predictable, meaningful growth is in your future. And with customer insight democratized, the customer's experience is owned by *everyone*, from the founders to the newest hire. Teams know the bar they'll be measured by, and more importantly, where that bar comes from: delivering customer value.

No more guessing. No more piecemeal tactics.

---

3   "Mastering the Art of the Outcome: How Guru Turned Customer Success Into a Company Cornerstone," The First Round, accessed January 6, 2023, https://review.firstround.com/ mastering-the-art-of-the-outcome-how-guru-turned-customer-success-into-a-company-cornerstone.

YOUR TURN

The biggest mistake you could make at this point would be to put all you've learned about your customer on a shelf. It's time to make your work compound by democratizing and integrating it across all teams.

1. Bring your top-priority customer Job and CX map to your team and gain maximum company-wide buy-in.
2. Identify the ways you can embed your new tools into your team's day-to-day work.
3. Iterate and expand on what the Customer-Led Growth Framework can do for your team, whether that's tackling new customer Jobs or supporting your efforts to move into new markets all together.

Find helpful guides and templates at forgetthefunnel.com/workbook.

Chapter 10

WHAT GOT YOU HERE WON'T GET YOU THERE

You came to this book because you're tired of guessing. You've tried what feels like *everything* to more predictably drive new traffic, leads, and signups. Maybe you've spent months working on content marketing and thought leadership pieces. Thrown money at paid social and search campaigns. Tweaked and optimized the funnel every way you can think of.

But *more* new tactics to generate *more* leads to bring in *more* sales reverts you back to marketing in a petri dish. Shots in the dark. Spaghetti. You remember the metaphors.

Bottom line: what got you to this point in your business won't get you to scalable, sustainable growth.

Figure 10.1. The phases and milestones of your customer's journey.

	Struggle		Evaluation		Growth	
	Problem	Interest	First Value	Value Realization	Continued Value	Value Growth
Thinking	"My clients are asking questions I can't answer." "Scraping Twitter is so time-consuming." "There has to be a better way."	"Will SparkToro be easier than my manual process?" "How much does it cost?" "The first free search is cool."	"What kind of time will I need to commit to learn SparkToro?" "Wow, I wouldn't have found these insights on my own."	"This will save me and my team so much time." "Now I can spend time crafting the perfect pitch, instead of figuring out WHO to pitch."	"I'm 3x faster than my previous method, and making 3x what I was before." "I can show my clients a better way to get the research they need done."	"I can offer audience research as an official service offering." "I want to expand my team and grow my audience research revenue."
Doing	Manually scraping social media Seeking help from colleagues on ways to go faster Searching for "audience research tools"	Visiting our website Looking at pricing First search Creating an account	Product tour Onboarding emails Trying new searches Clicking through profiles	Creating lists Comparing audiences Exporting data Upgrading from free	Creating new lists for each client's audience(s) Monitoring alerts and nudges to add new data to lists Receiving email that I'll soon exhaust searches	Receiving customer newsletter Submitting feature requests Receiving email asking for product reviews Telling friends and writing reviews
Feeling						

150 · FORGET THE FUNNEL

Up to now, you've *had* to guess, because the typical view of marketing as a "funnel" flattens your view of customers' *real* experience. It gives you a starting point, sure, but eventually it just muddies up which opportunities your team should really pursue.

That's why the Customer-Led Growth Framework requires you to *forget* **the funnel and see your customers as living, breathing, *whole* people you're in a meaningful relationship with.** Because you are.

Deconstructing the relationship you have with your customers into its critical parts, those leaps of faith, opens up a world of opportunity you wouldn't otherwise see. All the ways that their experience can be optimized and grow becomes available to you on a silver platter.

You'll know how to reach more of your best-fit customers. How to prove you understand them and the problem they need solving. How to help them reach value quickly and seamlessly with your product.

And though the easiest way to visualize this concept is by picturing a linear journey (Figure 10.1), it can help to think of your relationship with your customers as a *circle* rather than a line. If you run a recurring revenue business, you have nearly limitless potential to provide continued—and, ideally, *expanding*—customer value over time.

"Getting inside your best customers' heads" may not have sounded like a tangible solution to the enormous pressure you're feeling to hit your goals. **But now you understand that** it *is the key* to hitting your goals. No more wasting time, fumbling, *guessing*.

Once you've implemented the process laid out in this book, you'll have **confidence** in your marketing (and product, and sales) strategies to grow your business in both a sustainable and scalable way.

What got you here *in this book*, now **will** get you there.

You just have to start.

YOUR TURN

Get this book into the hands of the decision makers, team members, and practitioners who will champion this work forward.

Waiting just draws out the time your team is left doing their best with one hand tied behind their back—without the full understanding of your customers and their own critical role in customers' success.

We've made the Customer-Led Growth Framework and process as accessible as possible by making tools, templates, and checklists available to you. Please take advantage at forget-thefunnel.com/workbook.

ACKNOWLEDGMENTS

We owe so many people a huge thanks for their direct and indirect support of this book. Our own blood, sweat, and tears may have gone into writing it, but we didn't get here on our own. We stand humbly on the shoulders of giants.

Bob Moesta, thank you for believing in this project from the start, recognizing the need for this book to exist, and helping us get out of our own way.

Gail Fay and the whole team at Scribe, thank you for everything. Without your ability to get tricky concepts out of our heads and down on paper—as well as your extreme patience with us—we wouldn't be at this point.

Beth Thouin, Ethan Graham Roeder, and Zee Morandarte, you're what makes this whole thing more than just "the Claire and Gia show." Thank you endlessly for your collaboration, your intelligence, your humor, and for rolling (gracefully) with all of the punches.

To our earliest supporters and readers, thank you for your generous feedback. Your guidance was invaluable, and this book is so much better because of you. This includes Ramli John, Alli Blum, Asia Orangio, Kamil Rextin, Anand Thaker, Margaret Kelsey, Lucy Heskins, David Sherry, Brian Sun, Eric Tompkins, Krystyna Coyle, Masha Krol, Thorsten Bruchhaeuser, David Stanley, Alec Latimer, Mrig Pandey, and Helen Duffy—as well as all of the anonymous beta readers. We deeply appreciate all of your support.

To our Forget the Funnel community members, you've been on board the customer-led growth train before it even had that name! Thank you for your thought partnership, camaraderie, and mutual support over the years—and for weaving CLG into your own work to help countless companies be more customer-led.

Talia Wolf, Tara Robertson, Joanna Bain (Wiebe), April Dunford, Tiffany DaSilva, Els Aerts, Krista Seiden, Hana Abaza, and Angie Schottmuller, you've been here for us since day one. We couldn't have done *gestures at the past five years* without you.

To those directly and indirectly referenced in this book, including Tara Robertson, Luke Raynebeau, Lenny Rachitsky, Teresa Torres, Bobby Marhamat, Peter Polson, Andy Theimer, Sarah Boland, Gary Keller, Stephane Rivard, and Rick Nucci, thank you. Allison Esposito Medina, we wouldn't have met were it not for Tech Ladies! Chris Spiek, Jordan Skole, and the whole team at Autobooks, thanks for your trust and bravery throughout the process of testing some (very) unconventional emails. Rand Fishkin, Casey

Henry, and Amanda Natividad, you are the *best*. Thank you for your willingness to continually partner with us in fun, creative new ways.

GIA WOULD LIKE TO THANK:

My daughters, Lia and Kate. Though it'll be years before you know (or even care) what this book is about, on a million levels, I did this for you.

My husband, DJ. I don't know what I did to deserve you, but I'm grateful every single day. You're my Dead Sea.

My mother. For your spirit, fearlessness, and grit. You inspire me more than you know. My father. For your vision, hustle, and depth. You push me more than you know.

CLAIRE WOULD LIKE TO THANK:

My family. Mom and Dad: when the younger version of me received that opportunity to move across the country and stretch my world, you didn't stop me. I'm forever grateful.

Grammy, you inspire me. Thank you for enthusiastically supporting this project from the moment I shared the news with you.

Grandfather, I miss you often and like to think this would've made you proud.

I owe thanks to a long line of Suellentrops for my entrepreneurial spirit.

Stephen, how can I ever thank you enough? You are my person, and I am so grateful for how we've grown—*together.* I love you.

Blake, you may not have realized it, but your emotional support kept me going during some especially challenging phases of writing this book. To quote *Big Friendship:* "I love that you've known every version of me. You were there at the beginning and I want you there at the end."

Lastly, Gia: we fucking did it. Thank you for every single thing.

ABOUT THE AUTHORS

GEORGIANA LAUDI and **CLAIRE SUELLENTROP** co-founded Forget the Funnel, a consultancy that helps SaaS teams reach and retain high lifetime value customers.

Georgiana is a strategic advisor and speaker who's passionate about turning customer value into revenue-generating outcomes. Marketing online since 2000, she began her track record as a marketing executive and product growth advisor in 2010 working with high-growth, recurring-revenue startups.

Since 2014, Claire has helped SaaS companies grow to multi-millions in ARR by leveraging customer insights to fuel marketing and growth programs. She's spoken internationally about the impact of taking a customer-led approach, delivering presentations and training to audiences of founders, VC (venture capital)-backed teams, and enterprise executives.

Printed in Great Britain
by Amazon

34671403R00091